Words in Context

Thematischer Oberstufenwortschatz

von Bernhard Knop und
Corienne Naumann-Breeze

Ernst Klett Schulbuchverlag
Stuttgart Düsseldorf Berlin Leipzig

Words in Context, Thematischer Oberstufenwortschatz von Bernhard Knop und Corienne Naumann-Breeze.

Bildquellen
Barnaby's Picture Library: pp. 59, 117, 171
Camera Press: pp. 4, 125, 138
dpa: pp. 101, 143, 162
Picturepoint: pp. 63, 85, 177
Plantu: p. 106
Punch: pp. 78, 139

2. Auflage 2 5 4 3 2 | 1995 94 93 92 91

Alle Drucke dieser Auflage können im Unterricht nebeneinander benutzt werden.
Die letzte Zahl bezeichnet das Jahr dieses Druckes.

Umschlag: Manfred Muraro

Redaktion: Peter Holzke, Verlagsredakteur

Druck: Gutmann & Co., Heilbronn
ISBN 3-12-519610-8

Contents

HINWEISE FÜR DIE LERNENDEN

Der Untertitel „Thematischer Oberstufenwortschatz" sagt in stark verkürzter Form, was dieses Buch ist und was es Ihnen bietet:
Es ist vor allen Dingen ein Wortschatz, eine Sammlung von Vokabeln, die Sie benötigen, um über bestimmte Dinge zu lesen, zu sprechen oder zu schreiben.
Dieser Wortschatz wird jedoch nicht nur – wie in herkömmlichen Wortschätzen – in Listenform dargeboten. Vielmehr ist jedes Wort in einen sinnvollen Text eingebettet. Das erleichtert Ihnen nicht nur das Lernen und Behalten des Worts, sondern zeigt Ihnen zugleich seinen richtigen Gebrauch im Zusammenhang mit einem gegebenen Thema.
Die Auswahl der Themen orientiert sich an den Oberstufen-Lehrplänen der Bundesländer. Nicht jedes Thema wird für alle Schülerinnen und Schüler gleich wichtig sein, aber bei allen sollte man auch auf englisch mitreden können. Die meisten Fakten werden Ihnen aus dem Unterricht in anderen Fächern und aus Presse, Funk und Fernsehen geläufig sein, die passenden englischen Wörter dagegen lernen oder wiederholen Sie mit diesem Buch. Das heißt aber auch, daß keines der angegebenen Themen erschöpfend behandelt wird: Die Texte dienen lediglich dazu, den angemessenen Gebrauch der zu lernenden Wörter zu demonstrieren.
Wie arbeitet man mit dem „Thematischen Oberstufenwortschatz"? Wählen Sie einfach ein Thema, das Sie interessiert, oder das demnächst im Unterricht behandelt werden soll, oder das kürzlich besprochen wurde. Beim Durchlesen des Textes auf der linken Seite werden Sie die meisten Wörter aus dem Zusammenhang verstehen. Die genaue deutsche Entsprechung (bezogen auf diesen Kontext!) finden Sie gegenüber auf der rechten Seite, ebenso die korrekte Aussprache, soweit diese nicht selbstverständlich ist. Lesen Sie dann den Text oder Teile davon immer wieder einmal zwischendurch – auch beim Warten, in Bahn oder Bus, kurz bei jeder passenden Gelegenheit. So wird Ihnen der Fachwortschatz geläufig. Zur Kontrolle können Sie dann rechts die eine oder andere Spalte abdecken. So erkennen Sie, welches englische Wort Sie noch nicht zuverlässig verstehen, bzw. zu welchem deutschen Wort Ihnen der englische Ausdruck fehlt.
Während Sie sich auf diesem Wege das Schriftbild einprägen, ist das gegenseitige Abfragen hervorragend geeignet, zugleich die korrekte Aussprache und Betonung zu üben.
So gelangen Sie nach und nach und durch Ausnutzung von „toten" Zeiten zur sicheren Beherrschung des Wortschatzes, den Sie bei Klausuren, Referaten, im Abitur und vor allem im Gespräch mit Engländern und Amerikanern brauchen.

HINWEIS FÜR UNTERRICHTENDE

Offensichtlich ist die Behandlung eines Lehrplan-Themas auf der Oberstufe für Lehrer und Schüler sehr viel leichter, angenehmer und fruchtbringender, wenn wenig oder gar keine Zeit auf den Erwerb des Wortschatzes verwendet werden muß und man sich zügig den Inhalten zuwenden und diese stufengemäß diskutieren kann. Der thematische Oberstufenwortschatz schafft die Voraussetzung dafür: Geben Sie Ihren Kursteilnehmern rechtzeitig vorher – vielleicht schon am Beginn des Schul(halb)jahres – die Themen bekannt, mit denen die Schülerinnen und Schüler sich anhand dieses Buches vertraut machen sollen, damit sie für die Mitarbeit im Unterricht gerüstet sind.
Auch unterrichtsbegleitend und vor allen Dingen zum Wiederholen ist „Words in Context“ eine gute Hilfe.

Government and Politics

Basic information:

Unlike dictatorships, fascist and totalitarian regimes, democracy – or government by the people – requires a mandate from the majority of the electorate. This mandate is given in general elections and local (city and county council, borough) elections. As enlightened democracies have had universal suffrage for decades, every adult citizen, with only a few exceptions, is eligible to vote.

Elections are held at certain prescribed intervals, although a government may call a new election before the end of its official term of office. On Election Day the voters go to the polls to cast their votes for the candidates of their choice by placing their ballot-papers in the ballot-boxes at the polling-stations. After the votes have been counted it is usually

dictatorship	Diktatur
fascist/a fascist ['fæʃɪst]	faschistisch/ Faschist
regime [reɪ'ʒi:m]	Regime
democracy [dɪ'mɒkrəsɪ]	Demokratie
mandate ['mændeɪt]	Regierungsauftrag, Mandat
electorate [ɪ'lektərət]	Wählerschaft
general elections	allgemeine Wahlen
borough ['bʌrə]	Stadt-/Dorfgemeinde
enlightened	aufgeklärt
universal suffrage ['sʌfrɪdʒ]	allgemeines Wahlrecht
eligible ['elɪdʒəbl] **to vote**	wahl-, stimmberechtigt
interval ['ɪntəvl]	Abstand, Intervall
term of office	Amtszeit
voter	Wähler/in
to go to the polls [pəʊlz]	zur Wahl gehen
to cast one's vote	seine Stimme abgeben
ballot-paper	Stimmzettel
polling-station	Wahllokal

clear which party has won the election and can form a government: the one whose candidates have polled the majority of the votes over their opponents.

If the party in power up to an election is re-elected, it can stay in power, while the losing parties form the Opposition. A government without an overall majority usually decides to form a coalition, although there is no tradition of coalition governments in Britain and the USA. A party which has won the majority of the votes or even an overwhelming victory, a 'landslide' victory, can govern by itself. Should an elected representative resign or die, his or her successor is chosen in a by-election.

Government in Britain

The way to liberty and democracy in Britain was paved by Magna Carta in 1215. The present system of parliamentary democracy, combined with a constitutional monarchy, has proved an efficient way of conducting the nation's politics. Basically Britain has a two-party system: the Conservative (Tory) Party and the Labour Party. These parties' foreign, financial and domestic policies are discussed at party conferences. Although other smaller parties and splinter groups exist, their chances of winning an election are minimal because Britain has no proportional representation. The system of majority vote means that only the winning candidate and his or her party, the 'first past the post', profit from a victory in the constituency, as all the votes received by the losing candidate are 'wasted' votes.

A government may stay in office for a maximum period of five years, after which Parliament is dissolved by the sovereign and new elections take place. Parliament at Westminster is divided up into two Houses. The House of Lords (or Upper House), which can be described as politically conservative, has more than 1,000 members:

- the Lords Spiritual (archbishops and bishops),
- the Lords Temporal (life peers and hereditary peers) and
- the Law Lords.

Its Speaker is the Lord Chancellor, who is also a Cabinet Minister and the head of Britain's judiciary.

Although the House of Lords can hold up legislation and, together with the monarch, must approve a bill before it can become an act, it has little power in practice. It is the House of Commons, the Lower House, with its 650 Members of Parliament (MPs) representing the same number of constituencies, that is responsible for legislation. The main seat of political power and origin of most new bills is 10 Downing Street, the official

to poll [pəʊl]	erhalten, auf sich vereinigen
opponent [ə'pəʊnənt]	Gegner
overall majority	absolute Mehrheit
coalition [ˌkəʊə'lɪʃən]	Koalition
overwhelming	überwältigend
landslide	Erdrutsch
representative [ˌrepri'zentətɪv]	Abgeordnete(r)
to resign [ri'zaɪn]	zurücktreten
successor	Nachfolger/in
by-election	Nachwahl

monarchy ['mɒnəkɪ]	Monarchie
politics ['pɒlɪtɪks]	Politik
foreign policy	Außenpolitik
domestic policy	Innenpolitik
splinter group	Splittergruppe
proportional representation	Verhältniswahlrecht
majority vote	Mehrheitswahlrecht
first past the post	der erste im Ziel
constituency [kən'stɪtjʊənsɪ]	Wahlkreis
to dissolve [dɪ'zɒlv]	auflösen
sovereign ['sɒvrɪn]	Bezeichnung für den König, die Königin, Souverän
House of Lords	Oberhaus
Lords Spiritual	geistliche } – Mitglieder des Oberhauses
Lords Temporal	weltliche } – Mitglieder des Oberhauses
life peer	Mitglied des Oberhauses auf Lebenszeit
hereditary [hi'redɪtərɪ] **peer**	Mitglied des Oberhauses mit erblichem Titel
Law Lords	Mitglieder mit richterlicher Funktion
Speaker	Präsident/in des Oberhauses
Lord Chancellor	Lordkanzler
judiciary [dʒuː'dɪʃɪərɪ]	Gerichtswesen
legislation [ˌledʒɪs'leɪʃn]	Gesetzgebung
monarch ['mɒnək]	Monarch/in, Herrscher/in
bill	Gesetzesvorlage
act	(verabschiedetes) Gesetz
House of Commons	Unterhaus
Member of Parliament (MP)	Parlamentsabgeordnete(r)

residence of the Prime Minister. The Cabinet consists of the Prime Minister, who is appointed by the sovereign and is known as 'the first among equals', and of Cabinet Ministers chosen by the Prime Minister from the elected MPs.

Prominent politicians, including the Foreign Secretary, the Chancellor of the Exchequer, the Home Secretary, the Defence Secretary and leading members of the Opposition (above all the Shadow Cabinet) are known as front-benchers, while those without important positions are called back-benchers. The MPs with the most influence in the House of Commons are the Prime Minister, the Speaker and the Leader of the Opposition. Party discipline during debates and votes in Parliament is maintained by the party whips. Specialized work on complex policy issues is done by committees or subcommittees.

Regionalism and devolution

Regional differences of an economic nature have become so striking in the UK that the term 'North-South divide' is justified. In the North, especially in cities like Manchester, Liverpool and Newcastle-upon-Tyne, but also in Wales, Scotland and Northern Ireland, the unemployment rate is above average. This is mainly because heavy industry – the traditional coal-mining and shipbuilding industries – has declined and light industry, e.g. high-tech firms and important service industries, is mainly in the South.

Feeling neglected and ignored, the North accuses the government in London of being biased in favour of the South, which is better off economically. Especially in the 'Home Counties', those near or around London (e.g. Kent, Surrey, Sussex and Essex), average household incomes are higher, land and property values are so high, that there is a severe shortage of affordable housing, and the unemployment rate is relatively low.

Government measures have been launched aiming at closing the gap between the 'two nations' of Britain. Businesses and investors have been given more incentives to remain in the North.

Discontent with what is regarded by many Britons as centralized government has not only economic causes but also political and national ones. This explains the frequent demand for devolution, i.e. a decentralization of government and a transfer of legislative power from Westminster to directly elected regional assemblies in Scotland and Wales.

Prime Minister	Premierminister/in
politician [ˌpɒlɪˈtɪʃn]	Politiker/in
Foreign Secretary	Außenminister/in
Chancellor of the Exchequer [ɪksˈtʃekə]	Schatzkanzler/in, Finanzminister/in
Home Secretary	Innenminister/in
Shadow Cabinet	Schattenkabinett
Speaker	Präsident/in, Sprecher/in des Unterhauses
vote	Abstimmung
whip	parlamentarischer Geschäftsführer
issue [ˈɪʃjuː]	Problem, Streitfrage
committee [kəˈmɪtɪ]	Ausschuß
subcommittee	Unterausschuß
regionalism [ˈriːdʒənəlɪzəm]	Betonung der Sonderinteressen einzelner Landesteile, Regionalismus
devolution [diːvəˈluːʃən]	Dezentralisierung der polit. Macht
divide	Kluft
heavy industry	Schwerindustrie
high-tech [-tek]	hochtechnologisch
service	Dienstleistungs-
to neglect	vernachlässigen
to be biased [ˈbaɪəst] **in favour of**	voreingenommen sein zugunsten von
county	Grafschaft
property	*hier:* Immobilien-
affordable [əˈfɔːdəbl]	erschwinglich
housing	*hier:* Wohnraum
gap	Kluft, Abstand
investor	Geld-, Kapitalanleger/in
incentive	Anreiz
discontent [dɪskənˈtent]	Unzufriedenheit
transfer [ˈtrænsfɜː]	Übertragung, Verlagerung
assembly	beratende oder gesetzgebende Körperschaft

Right-wing and left-wing policies

Typical policies pursued by basically right-wing parties like the British Conservative Party include:
- a free-enterprise economy with state intervention only where necessary
- privatization (denationalization) wherever possible
- tight control of the money supply to fight inflation
- no subsidies for ailing industries

Predominantly left-wing parties like the British Labour Party are in favour of:
- a more mixed economy: a free-enterprise system but with more government control
- partial renationalization (or at least no further privatization)
- workers' participation
- more job-creation programmes and social welfare programmes

Government in the US

The backbones of US democracy and the system of federal government are the Declaration of Independence (1776) and the Constitution of the USA (1787) with its seven original articles and twenty-six amendments. The Constitution prescribes that federal power should be shared by the three 'separate but equal' branches of government:
- the legislative branch (Congress)
- the executive branch (the Administration)
- the judicial branch (the Supreme Court)

A possible abuse of power or infringement by any one branch of the rights and duties of the others is prevented by a system of checks and balances. This separation of powers applies not only at a national level but also at a state level; each state has its own written constitution, its executive branch headed by the governor, its state senate and its own courts.

The Congress is bicameral, consisting of two Houses or chambers, the Senate and the House of Representatives. The Senate has 100 Senators (two from each state), who are elected for a six-year term. Its leader is the Vice-President, who, however, only has a vote if the Senate vote is split down the middle (50:50).

At its highest level, the executive branch is represented by the Administration, consisting of the President (whose additional titles are Commander-in-Chief and Head of State), the Vice-President and the Cabinet

right-wing policies	rechte Politik
left-wing policies	linke Politik
to pursue [pə'sju:]	*hier:* betreiben, verfolgen
free-enterprise economy	freie Marktwirtschaft
intervention	Eingriff, Intervention
privatization [ˌpraɪvɪtaɪ'zeɪʃən]	Privatisierung
money supply	Geldumlauf
subsidies ['sʌbsɪdɪz] *pl*	Subventionen
ailing	notleidend, kränkelnd
renationalization	Wiederverstaatlichung
workers' participation	Mitbestimmung
job-creation programme	Arbeitsplatzbeschaffungsprogramm
social welfare programme	Sozialhilfeprogramm

backbone	Rückgrat
federal	Bundes-
Constitution	Verfassung
article	Artikel, Paragraph (eines Gesetzes)
amendment	Zusatz (zur Verfassung)
separate ['seprət]	getrennt
branch	Zweig
legislative ['ledʒɪslətɪv]	gesetzgebend
Congress ['kɒŋgres]	Kongreß
executive [ˌɪg'zekjʊtiv]	ausführend
Administration *(BE:* Government)	*hier:* Regierung
judicial [dʒu'dɪʃl]	rechtsprechend
Supreme [sʊ'prɪ:m] **Court**	Oberstes Bundesgericht in den USA
abuse [ə'bju:s]	Mißbrauch
infringement [ɪn'frɪndʒmənt]	Verletzung, Übergriff
checks and balances	System der gegenseitigen Kontrolle (Gewaltenteilung)
governor	Gouverneur
bicameral [baɪ'kæmərəl]	aus zwei Kammern bestehend
chamber ['tʃeɪmbə]	Kammer
Senate ['senɪt]	Senat
House of Representatives	Abgeordnetenhaus
term	*hier:* Amtszeit
Vice-President [vaɪs-]	Vizepräsident/in
Commander-in-Chief	Oberbefehlshaber/in der Streitkräfte
head of state	Staatsoberhaupt

appointed by the President. Its seat is the White House in Washington, D.C. Unlike British Cabinet Ministers, US Administration members – the Secretary of State, the Treasury Secretary, the Defense Secretary, the Interior Secretary etc. – do not need to have been elected by the people, although the Senate must consent to their appointments.

The President can exercise his power of veto to prevent the passing of a bill, but vetoed bills approved by a two-thirds majority in both Houses can still become Acts of Congress.

The leading representative of the judicial branch of government is the Supreme Court, the highest court of appeal. Its task is to interpret the Constitution and ensure that legislation is constitutional. The nine judges, headed by the Chief Justice, are appointed by the President for life. They can declare existing laws to be unconstitutional and have been responsible for many landmark decisions that have changed the face of American society.

Presidential elections

The President serves a four-year term and may stay in office for a total of two full terms only. He or she must be an American citizen born in the USA and over 35 years of age. Each of the two parties – the Republican Party and the Democratic Party – must choose a nominee from the various aspiring candidates. The presidential and vice-presidential nominees are selected at the parties' national conventions by a simple majority of the delegates previously chosen either at state conventions and caucuses or elected in primaries.

After the official nomination the election campaign begins in earnest, continuing until Election Day, the Tuesday after the first Monday in November in leap years. Voters are registered and the party machinery drums up support, tries to win floating voters over etc.

On Election Day the electorate votes not for the presidential candidates themselves but for those presidential electors (members of the Electoral College) who have pledged their support to a particular candidate.

The officially elected President, who is inaugurated and sworn in in January, is the candidate who has received the votes of the majority of electors in the Electoral College.

Secretary of State *(AE)*	Außenminister/in
Treasury ['treʒərɪ] **Secretary** *(AE)*	Finanzminister/in
Defense Secretary *(AE)*	Verteidigungsminister/in
Interior [ɪn'tɪərɪə] **Secretary** *(AE)*	Innenminister/in
to consent to	zustimmen
power of veto ['vi:təʊ]	Einspruchsrecht
to veto	Veto einlegen gegen
bill	Gesetzesvorlage
act	(verabschiedetes) Gesetz
court of appeal	Berufungs-, Appellationsgericht
constitutional	verfassungsmäßig
chief justice	oberster Richter/in
for life	auf Lebenszeit
unconstitutional	verfassungswidrig
landmark decision	eine Entscheidung, die als Markstein/ Wendepunkt zu betrachten ist

nominee [nɒmɪ'ni:]	(offizieller) Kandidat/in
aspiring	ehrgeizig
convention	Versammlung, Parteitag
caucus ['kɔ:kəs]	Vorversammlung von Wählern zur Vorbereitung einer Wahl und Ernennung eines Kandidaten
primary ['praɪmərɪ]	Vorwahl
election campaign	Wahlkampf
leap year	Schaltjahr
to register ['redʒɪstə]	*hier:* auf eine Wahlliste setzen
party machinery	Parteiorganisation
floating voter	Wechselwähler/in
presidential electors	Wahlmänner bei einer Präsidentschaftswahl
Electoral College	Wahlmännergremium
to pledge	geloben, sich verpflichten
to inaugurate [ɪ'nɔ:gjʊreɪt]	feierlich in ein Amt einführen
to be sworn in	vereidigt werden

Background USA

The growth of a nation

In 1607 Jamestown, Virginia, became the first English colony to be established in the New World. The 'Pilgrim Fathers', including Puritan refugees in search of religious freedom, arrived in Plymouth in the 'Mayflower' in 1620. These 'Pilgrim Fathers' and some other English settlers, who subsequently founded the colony of Massachusetts, signed the 'Mayflower Compact' in 1620. This document was the blueprint for the establishment of a 'civil Body Politick', a community whose citizens could live in keeping with democratic principles and still remain loyal subjects of the reigning British monarch. Other British dissenters soon followed: English Roman Catholics founded Maryland in 1634, English Quakers Pennsylvania in 1682. By 1775 there were already thirteen Eng-

Pilgrim Fathers	Pilgerväter
refugee [refjʊ'dʒiː]	Flüchtling
settler	Siedler/in
compact	Abkommen, Vertrag
blueprint	*hier:* Plan, Entwurf
body politick ['pɒlɪtɪk] *archaic*	Staatskörper
subject	Untertan
to reign [reɪn]	regieren, herrschen
monarch ['mɒnək]	Monarch/in, Herrscher/in
dissenter	Andersdenkende/r, Dissident/in

lish colonies spread along the Atlantic seaboard and inhabited mainly by colonists of British stock.

The Declaration of Independence was adopted on July 4, 1776 (now called Independence Day). This document emphasizes that all citizens have 'unalienable Rights', including 'Life, Liberty and the Pursuit of Happiness'. The people have the right 'to alter or to abolish' any government hindering the achievement of these goals.

In 1783 Britain officially declared the former colonies independent in the Treaty of Paris. The new republic was now free to govern itself and to draft its own constitution, which came into effect in 1789.

The pioneers and the land

A time of expansion now began: fearless frontiersmen passed beyond one frontier after another and the pioneer spirit sent settlers further and further west in trains of covered wagons. New territory was gradually opened up, land was cleared and cultivated and settlements and townships were established as far as the Pacific coast.

The difficulties that had to be overcome helped to mould the American character and determine American life-styles and values: a community spirit and neighbourliness on the one hand, self-help, self-reliance, individualism, initiative and an entrepreneurial spirit on the other.

The huge dimensions and geographical diversity of the land also proved a great challenge: mountainous regions (the Rockies in the West, the Appalachians in the East), the subtropical climate of the Southern states, the barren plateaus and deserts in Arizona, the fertile prairies and vast central plains, the swamps of Florida etc.

seaboard	Küste
stock	Abstammung, Herkunft
Declaration of Independence	Unabhängigkeitserklärung
to adopt	annehmen
unalienable/inalienable [–'eɪljənəbl]	unveräußerlich
pursuit [pə'sju:t] **of happiness**	Streben nach Glück
to abolish [ə'bɒlɪʃ]	abschaffen
goal	Ziel
treaty	Vertrag
to draft	aufsetzen, entwerfen
constitution	Verfassung
to come into effect	in Kraft treten, gültig werden

expansion [ɪk'spænʃn]	Ausbreitung
frontiersman [frʌn'tɪəzmən]	Grenzer, Grenzbewohner, -ansiedler
frontier	Grenzland, Gebiet an der Siedlungsgrenze
covered wagon	Planwagen
to open up	erschließen
to clear	*hier:* roden
to cultivate	(Land) bestellen
to mould	formen, bilden, gestalten
community spirit	Gemeinschaftsgeist
neighbourliness	gutnachbarliches Verhalten
self-reliance	Selbständigkeit, Selbstvertrauen
entrepreneurial [ˌɒntrəprə'nɜ:rɪəl] **spirit**	Unternehmergeist
diversity [daɪ'vɜ:sətɪ]	Vielfalt
challenge	Herausforderung
barren ['bærən]	unfruchtbar, öde
plateau ['plætəʊ]	Hochebene
desert ['dezət]	Wüste
fertile ['fɜ:taɪl]	fruchtbar
plain	Ebene
swamp [swɒmp]	Sumpf, Sumpfland

Immigration and assimilation

For the colonists the American dream had largely been realized: they were free from absolutism and religious persecution and were the masters of their own destiny. Shortly after the founding of the republic, poor and oppressed people from Northern and Western Europe (the 'old immigrants') began to immigrate to the US. They all wished to benefit from the 'unlimited opportunities'. The US had little difficulty in assimilating these immigrants.

Problems began to arise when the 'new immigrants', who arrived from the latter part of the 19th century on, included Jews fleeing from pogroms in Poland and Russia, Irish Catholics fleeing from famines, Greek and Russian members of the Orthodox Church etc. It was not as easy for these new immigrants to blend with the resident population.

Nevertheless immigration remained unrestricted until the Immigration Act of 1924 introduced a quota system with a clear bias in favour of immigrants from Northern and Western Europe.

It is no longer common to speak of the US as a melting pot, in which the mingling of different nationalities, races and religions would produce 'a new race, a new religion, a new state'. On the contrary, the advantages of cultural pluralism have become increasingly evident. Provided all immigrants adapt to a certain accepted code of behaviour, or, simply, act like Americans, there is no reason why they should not preserve their own culture, religion and ethnic identities. Even those whose physical appearance is strikingly different and who could never really melt biologically – Asians and Blacks – can be just as 'American' as WASPs (White Anglo-Saxon Protestants) or 'hyphenated Americans' (Italo-Americans etc).

Thus the ideal of American society as a melting pot has been replaced by that of a 'salad bowl'.

The Hispanics

The Hispanics are a good example of an ethnic group that has maintained its own culture, language and (Roman Catholic) religion. Most Hispanics wish to uphold the standards and values of their own culture and avoid losing their identity in the mainstream of US society. They have been assimilated neither culturally nor socially.

Many Hispanics concentrated in the large urban areas of California, New York, Texas and Florida are discriminated against, often overtly. Although there are some bilingual schools, they are underprivileged in the

persecution	Verfolgung
destiny ['destɪnɪ]	Schicksal
to oppress	unterdrücken
to immigrate	einwandern
unlimited opportunities	unbegrenzte Möglichkeiten
to assimilate	aufnehmen, anpassen
pogrom ['pɒgrəm]	Pogrom, (Juden-)Verfolgung
famine ['fæmɪn]	Hungersnot
to blend	sich vermischen, sich harmonisch verbinden
act	Gesetz
quota	*hier:* Einwanderungsquote
bias ['baɪəs]	Neigung
melting pot	Schmelztiegel
to mingle	verschmelzen, sich verbinden
pluralism	Vielheit, Pluralismus
evident	offensichtlich
to adapt to	sich anpassen an
code of behaviour	Verhaltenskodex
ethnic	völkisch
identity [aɪ'dentətɪ]	Charakter, Eigenheit, Identität
to melt	verschmelzen, sich vermischen
Asian ['eɪʃən]	Asiate/Asiatin
hyphenated ['haɪfəneɪtəd]	mit einem Bindestrich versehen
salad bowl [bəʊl]	Salatschüssel
Hispanic [hɪ'spænɪk]	US-Bürger/in spanischer Kultur
to uphold	aufrechterhalten, behalten
mainstream	*hier:* die breite Masse
to discriminate against someone	jemanden benachteiligen
overt ['əʊvɜːt]	offen(kundig)
bilingual [baɪ'lɪŋgwəl]	zweisprachig

field of education as well as in housing and employment. While illegal immigrants exploited by unscrupulous employers are clearly worst off, a high percentage even of second-generation legal immigrants are unemployed and forced to live in substandard housing.

As they are under-represented in town councils, school boards etc., they have little say in American politics.

The South

The South of the USA is normally associated with the former slave-holding states, in which blacks toiled on the cotton plantations of rich and conservative white landowners, with the Civil War, with a hot and humid climate, flat country, large and flourishing cities like Dallas, Houston or Atlanta or tourist resorts in the sunshine state of Florida, to list only some of the more familiar features.

Historical outline:

The Civil War (1861–1865) broke out when the Confederacy (the eleven Confederate States) in the South jointly decided to secede from the Union in order to maintain their states' rights and uphold the institution of slavery. The industrialized Northern states, which were determined to preserve the Union, eventually won the war and subsequently subjected the South to rigorous federal control from Washington. The conquered South was treated as if it had been a foreign enemy and, during 'Reconstruction', the period of occupation and reform after the war, many changes were forced on it. As the North was opposed to slavery, the slaves on the plantations were emancipated in 1865.

The North prospered, the South remained for decades a rural, backward region.

The situation today:

The South has meanwhile been fully integrated into the US in political, economic, legal and social respects, so that there is now little resemblance between the 'new' and the 'old' South. Thanks to such legislation as the 1954 Act which declared racial segregation in schools unconstitutional and the Civil Rights Act of 1964, which outlawed racial discrimination, attitudes to and treatment of blacks have changed so much that problems related to the race question and segregation are now no

housing	*hier:* Wohnverhältnisse
to exploit	ausbeuten
unscrupulous [ʌn'skru:pjʊləs]	skrupellos
second-generation immigrants	in den USA geborene Kinder von Einwanderern
substandard	minderwertig
housing	*hier:* Wohnung(en)
town council	Stadtrat
school board	Schulkommission, Schulamt
to have little say	wenig Einfluß haben

to toil	hart arbeiten, 'schuften'
cotton	Baumwolle
plantation	Plantage
Civil War	Bürgerkrieg
humid ['hju:mɪd]	feucht
flourishing ['flʌrɪʃɪŋ]	blühend, gedeihend

the Confederacy [kən'fedərəsɪ]	Konföderation der US-Südstaaten
to secede [sɪ'si:d]	abtrünnig werden, abfallen
to maintain	*hier:* behalten
to preserve	bewahren, erhalten
rigorous ['rɪgərəs]	streng
federal	Bundes-
to conquer ['kɒŋkə]	besiegen, unterwerfen
occupation	Besatzung
to emancipate	befreien, freilassen
to prosper ['prɒspər]	gedeihen
rural ['rʊərəl]	ländlich
backward ['bækwəd]	rückständig

to integrate	eingliedern, integrieren
resemblance	Ähnlichkeit
racial segregation	Rassentrennung
unconstitutional	verfassungswidrig
civil rights	Bürgerrechte
act	Gesetz
to outlaw	*hier:* verbieten

greater in the South than elsewhere in the US. Examples of far-reaching changes that have taken place include:

- a growth in the population of the South as a result of migration from the North-East
- urban development leading to a growth in the size of Southern cities
- industrial expansion thanks to a steady increase in the number of industries setting up plants in the South
- the conversion of farms into automated agribusinesses, in which large sums of money have been invested.

US world leadership

Since World War II the US has been the leader of the Western world and a dominant world power in both economic and military respects. Its main rival in postwar years for political and military hegemony worldwide has been the Soviet Union.

The end of World War II marked the beginning of the Cold War, an era of military tension between the US and the USSR. During the subsequent decades of hostility the US was committed to building up a defence system worldwide and making treaties with its allies in the West.

As each of the two superpowers aimed at achieving military superiority, an arms race began and preparations were made for the eventuality of conventional, biological and chemical warfare. A policy of nuclear deterrence led to the creation of huge stockpiles of nuclear weaponry.

Since the period of détente began in the seventies, hostility and tension have lessened noticeably and the first steps towards disarmament have been taken. The improvement of Soviet-American relations – thanks to the SALT treaties and summit conferences – has made a lasting peaceful co-existence seem possible.

The scepticism, pessimism and lack of self-confidence resulting from the Vietnam War have now been replaced by a resurgence of national pride, patriotism and optimism in the US. Economic competition rather than military confrontation is the main concern of the superpowers today.

As a result of the uprisings in the former Soviet satellites behind the Iron Curtain – East Germany, Poland, Hungary etc. – in 1989, the monolithic structure of the Soviet bloc, even of the USSR itself, has been replaced to a large extent by political pluralism, economic reforms and an increase in national autonomy.

migration	Wanderung
urban development	Stadtentwicklung
expansion [ɪk'spænʃən]	Ausdehnung, Ausweitung
plant	Fabrik
conversion	Umwandlung
automated	automatisiert
agribusiness	'Agrarfabrik'
to invest	investieren
dominant	beherrschend
rival [raɪvl]	Rivale/Rivalin, Konkurrent/in
hegemony [hɪ'gemənɪ]	politische Vormachtstellung
era ['ɪərə]	Zeitalter, Ära
tension	Spannung(en)
to be committed	festgelegt sein, verpflichtet sein
treaty	Vertrag
ally ['ælaɪ]	Verbündete(r)
superiority [su:ˌpɪərɪ'ɒrətɪ]	Überlegenheit
arms race	Wettrüsten
warfare	Kriegführung
nuclear deterrence	nukleare Abschreckung
stockpile of nuclear weaponry	Kernwaffenarsenal
détente [deɪ'tɑ:nt]	Entspannung
disarmament	Abrüstung
SALT (Strategic Arms Limitation Talks)	Verhandlungen über die Begrenzung strategischer Waffen
summit conference	Gipfeltreffen
resurgence [rɪ'sɜ:dʒəns]	Wiederaufleben
competition	Wettstreit, -bewerb
confrontation	feindliche Gegenüberstellung
uprising	Aufstand
satellite	*hier:* Satellitenstaat, abhängiger Staat
Iron Curtain	Eiserner Vorhang
monolithic	gigantisch, monolithisch
pluralism	Vielfalt
autonomy [ɔ:'tɒnəmɪ]	Selbständigkeit, Autonomie

The overthrow of Communist governments, the successful popular demand for democratically elected governments and various Western freedoms and rights as well as the rejection of the planned economy system in favour of free enterprise have already changed the face of Central and Eastern Europe.

Communism and Soviet expansionism are now therefore no longer the main concerns of US foreign policy. The bipolar world dominated by two military blocs, NATO and the Warsaw Pact, is now in a state of flux. The preservation of peace is dependent on the restructuring of hitherto existing alliances and the creation of a new security framework.

overthrow	Sturz
popular	*hier:* vom Volke ausgehend
rejection	Ablehnung, Zurückweisung
planned economy	Planwirtschaft
free enterprise	freie Marktwirtschaft
expansionism [ɪk'spænʃənɪzəm]	Expansionspolitik
bipolar [baɪ'pəʊlə]	mit 2 gegensätzlichen Polen versehen, bipolar
NATO (North Atlantic Treaty Organization)	Nato (Nordatlantikpakt)
Warsaw ['wɔ:sɔ:] **Pact**	Warschauer Pakt
flux	Wandel
restructuring	Neu-, Umgestaltung
alliance	Bündnis, Allianz
framework	Rahmen, System, Gefüge

Civil war in Northern Ireland

Fresh wave of IRA violence

Ulster Catholics still face bias in their search for jobs

Is there a solution to the conflict?

The Conflict in Northern Ireland

Basic information:

Northern Ireland has been part of the United Kingdom (UK) since 1921, when Ireland was partitioned, the southern part becoming the Irish Free State (later called the Republic of Ireland). About two thirds of the population of Northern Ireland or Ulster (the name of the six counties) are Protestant and one third Catholic.

The IRA (Irish Republican Army), a terrorist underground organization, aims at the reunification of Ireland (its members are 'Republicans' or 'Nationalists'). Its political wing is known as Sinn Fein.

The Protestants also have radical, extremist parties or organizations like the Ulster Unionists (who want to maintain Ulster's union with Britain at all costs) or the Ulster Freedom Fighters (UFF), a paramilitary terrorist organization. Each side is regularly provoked by terrorist attacks launched by the other side.

The roots of the religious conflict lie in the social discrimination against the Catholics by the Protestants: the Catholics complain about the unfair

civil war Bürgerkrieg
IRA (Irish Republican Army) radikale Untergrundorganisation der katholischen Minderheit Nordirlands
Ulster ['ʌlstə] informeller Name für Nordirland
bias ['baɪəs] Vorurteil, Voreingenommenheit

to partition [pɑ:'tɪʃn] teilen

county Grafschaft

reunification [ˌri:ju:nɪfɪ'keɪʃn] Wiedervereinigung
Sinn Fein ['ʃɪn'feɪn] 'we ourselves', politischer Flügel der IRA
to maintain aufrechterhalten
paramilitary halb-, paramilitärisch
to provoke provozieren
to launch an attack angreifen
discrimination against Benachteiligung von

employment practices of Protestant private or public-sector companies. They demand legislation to tackle sectarian discrimination in employment (by monitoring the religious composition of the workforce) and to guarantee equal job opportunities.

The "Irish Question" (the conflict between the Protestant majority and the Catholic minority in Ulster) is further complicated by the economic difference between the two parts of Ireland – Northern Ireland, which is relatively prosperous, and the Republic of Ireland, which is one of the poorest countries in Europe. This explains why many people in Ulster, even Catholics, want to retain their union with Great Britain.

Historical reasons for the conflict:

The conflict between the Irish and the British dates back many centuries:

1167 – Anglo-Norman invaders try to gain control of most of Ireland but with little success: English rule does not extend beyond the area around Dublin

1536 – Henry VIII's attempt to impose the Reformation on the Irish remains unsuccessful (the origin of the religious conflict)

1607 – the Irish Catholic chieftains are defeated and in the following years Protestant settlers, mostly Scottish Protestant farmers, come from Britain to Ulster in what is called the 'Plantation of Ulster' (the origin of the Ulster problem)

1690 – William of Orange defeats the Catholics in the Battle of the Boyne. This battle becomes the symbol of Protestant supremacy (celebration of 'Orange Day')

1800 – After the failure of the rebellion of the 'United Irishmen' in 1798, British power is soon consolidated by the abolition of the Irish Parliament in the Act of Union of 1801

1912 – Units of Ulster Volunteers are formed by Northern Protestants to resist the Home Rule Bill, which would have created an independent Ireland

1921 – The island is partitioned: an Irish Free State (Eire) is formed, and Northern Ireland (the six Ulster counties belonging to the United Kingdom) comes into existence

1949 – The 'Irish Free State' leaves the Commonwealth and becomes the 'Republic of Ireland'

1969 – in Northern Ireland, a Civil Rights Movement on the Catholic side meets with resistance from extremist Protestants; British troops are sent to Northern Ireland and intervene to maintain law and order in the troubled province

the public sector	der öffentliche Dienst
public-sector *adj*	zum öffentlichen Dienst gehörig
legislation [ˌledʒɪsˈleɪʃn]	Gesetzgebung
sectarian	konfessionell (bedingt)
to monitor	überwachen
composition	Zusammensetzung
workforce	Arbeitnehmerschaft, Belegschaft
equal job opportunities	Chancengleichheit am Arbeitsplatz
prosperous [ˈprɒspərəs]	wohlhabend
to retain	bewahren
to date back	zurückgehen
century	Jahrhundert
invader	Eindringling
to impose on	auferlegen, aufdrängen
chieftain [ˈtʃiːftən]	Häuptling
supremacy [sʊˈpreməsɪ]	Vorherrschaft
abolition [ˌæbəʊˈlɪʃn]	Abschaffung, Beseitigung
Eire [ˈɛərə]	gälischer Name für Irland
civil rights movement	Bürgerrechtsbewegung
to intervene	eingreifen, intervenieren

Recent developments:

The Northern Ireland government and parliament ('Stormont') and the British troops were unable to control the troubles and solve the conflict, so the British Government in Westminster (London) dissolved Stormont and assumed responsibility for governing Ulster ('Direct Rule') in 1972. However, the troubles have continued. Even the Anglo-Irish Agreement of 1985, in which the Republic of Ireland was granted a say in the affairs of Northern Ireland, has done little to reduce the violence in Ulster.

No solution to the conflict is in sight and the chances of peace are as remote as ever.

Radical Catholics say:

1. We have suffered from the consequences of English conquest and oppression for several hundred years. Today the British practise 'neo-colonialism'. Their troops are an army of occupation.
2. We are under-represented in social and political fields and discriminated against in housing, employment etc.
3. The IRA is a genuine political movement with Sinn Fein as its political mouthpiece. It represents the opinions of large sections of the population.
4. We are fighting for a just cause: that of expelling the British from Ulster and of reunifying Ireland under Catholic rule.
5. The more of us are killed by British soldiers or the Ulster police forces, the more martyrs are created; each time there are more of us ready to revenge their deaths. The 'armed struggle' of the IRA causes bloodshed and human suffering, but these are unavoidable consequences of the fight for self-determination.

Means of IRA protest:

1. burning tyres in the streets, blocking roads with burning vehicles,
2. stoning police patrols, sniping at the security forces,
3. hijacking vehicles, placing bombs in them and driving them to designated targets (army barracks, police stations, or pubs frequented by British soldiers),

4 going on hunger strikes and, by dying of starvation as some detained IRA terrorists have done, becoming martyrs in the eyes of other terrorists.

to dissolve [dɪ'zɒlv]	auflösen
to grant a say	Mitspracherecht gewähren
remote	entfernt
conquest ['kɒŋkwest]	Eroberung
oppression	Unterdrückung
neo-colonialism [ˌni:əʊkə'ləʊn-jəlɪzəm]	Neokolonialismus
occupation [ɒkjʊ'peɪʃən]	Besatzung
under-represented	zu schwach vertreten, unterrepräsentiert
housing	Wohnverhältnisse
mouthpiece	Sprachrohr
just	gerecht
to expel [ɪk'spel]	vertreiben, verbannen
martyr ['mɑ:tə]	Märtyrer/in
to revenge	rächen
bloodshed ['blʌdʃed]	Blutvergießen
self-determination	Selbstbestimmung
patrol [pə'trəʊl]	Patrouille
to snipe	aus dem Hinterhalt schießen
sniper	Heckenschütze/-schützin
security forces	Sicherheitskräfte
to hijack	entführen
target ['tɑ:gɪt]	Ziel, Zielscheibe
barracks *sing. + pl.*	Kaserne
to detain	in Untersuchungshaft (be)halten, festhalten

Extremist Protestants say:

1. The IRA glorifies death, violence, blood and sacrifice; our counter-attacks are only a reaction to their terror; IRA terror tactics are condemned worldwide; we refuse to give in to IRA terrorism.
2. If the British troops withdraw, there will be even more turmoil and bloodshed.
3. Ulster is British; most of us are descendants of the English or Scottish planters of the 17th century; we have the same right to our (Protestant) homeland as the descendants of the (more recent) settlers in the USA or Australia have to their native countries.

Possible solutions:

1. If the 'armed struggle' between the two sides does not cease, bitterness will grow and the attacks will become more savage and brutal; as the cycle of violence cannot be allowed to continue indefinitely, a political solution must be found.
2. Sectarian discrimination in employment must be made illegal; the religious composition of the employees in companies or in the public sector must be monitored to ensure a fair representation of Catholics.
3. If the IRA were really invincible, it might prove wiser to come to terms with it.
4. The areas in which the majority of the inhabitants resent being part of the UK could be ceded to the Republic of Ireland.
5. The reunification of the two parts of Ireland with guaranteed minority rights for the Protestants.
6. The separation of Northern Ireland from the UK and its existence as an independent state.
7. The replacement of the British troops by UN troops.

to glorify	verherrlichen
to condemn [kən'dem]	verurteilen
to give in to …	sich von … geschlagen geben
to withdraw	(sich) zurückziehen
turmoil ['tɜ:mɔɪl]	Aufruhr, Unruhe
descendant [dɪ'sendənt]	Nachkomme
planter	Pflanzer, Siedler
native	*hier:* Heimat-
to cease [si:s]	aufhören
savage ['sævɪdʒ]	grausam, brutal
cycle	Kreis(lauf), Zyklus
employee [ˌemplɔɪ'i:]	Arbeitnehmer/in, Angestellte(r)
to ensure [ɪn'ʃʊə]	sicherstellen
invincible	unbesiegbar
to come to terms with	sich einigen mit, sich arrangieren mit
to resent [rɪ'zent]	sich ärgern über, übelnehmen
to cede	abtreten, abgeben, überlassen

The British Empire The Common-wealth

The British Empire

The claim that the sun never set on the British Empire was not an empty boast. By the end of the nineteenth century the Empire included nearly a quarter of the earth's land surface and more than a quarter of its population.

This imperial endeavour began with the foundation of the first English colony in America in 1607 and ended when British India became independent and was partitioned into Pakistan and India in 1947.

The thirteen American colonies, the so-called First Empire, were lost in the War of American Independence (1775–83). Commercial expansionism and the acquisition of new territories were the motives for the

empire	Weltreich
boast	Prahlerei
imperial	das britische Weltreich betreffend
endeavour [ɪn'devə]	Bemühung, Anstrengung
to partition [pɑ:'tɪʃn]	teilen
expansionism [ɪk'spænʃənɪzəm]	Expansionspolitik
acquisition	Erwerb
territory	Gebiet, Territorium

creation of the Second Empire, which reached its zenith in the 19th century when Queen Victoria was proclaimed Empress of India in 1877. By then Burma, Ceylon and much of the West Indies had already been brought under British sovereignty and the Antipodes – Australia and New Zealand – had been colonized by British settlers. In 1867 Canada became the Empire's first self-governing dominion.

In the late 19th century the Empire-builders turned their attention to the 'dark continent' of Africa, although trade settlements had already existed in Gambia and on the Gold Coast for three centuries and the interior had already been penetrated by explorers and missionaries. In addition to the Union of South Africa, granted dominion status in 1910, many African Crown Colonies and protectorates were established and settled by British farmers.

Since granting these countries their independence in the 1950s and 1960s, Britain has retained only few vestiges of imperial power: dependencies of the Crown such as Hong Kong, Gibraltar, the Falkland Islands etc. The transformation of the British Empire into the Commonwealth began with the Statute of Westminster (1931), which refers to a free association of self-governing countries equal in rank and united by a common allegiance to the Crown.

The Commonwealth

The terms Commonwealth or Commonwealth of Nations refer to a voluntary association of 49 independent states with a combined population of some 1,200 million (nearly a quarter of the world's total). In the course of decolonization between 1947 and 1972 many former colonies emerged as new nations in Africa, Asia, the Pacific and the Caribbean. On attaining independence, most decided to join the Commonwealth, though some countries have since left for various reasons.

The main characteristic of the Commonwealth is its diversity. It includes a whole continent (Australia), large countries like Canada and India and small islands such as Antigua and Barbados.

Distributed over all continents, it is multi-racial, with a wide range of cultures, languages, nationalities and faiths. Most members, apart from some exceptions like Singapore and the 'White Commonwealth' (the United Kingdom, Canada, Australia and New Zealand), belong to the Third World. Queen Elizabeth II is recognized by the inhabitants of Commonwealth countries as head of the Commonwealth.

zenith ['zenɪθ]	Höhepunkt, Zenit
to proclaim	*hier:* ausrufen
empress/emperor	Kaiserin/Kaiser
sovereignty ['sɒvrəntɪ]	Landeshoheit
antipodes [æn'tɪpədi:z]	diametral gegenüberliegende Teile der Erde
to colonize	besiedeln
dominion	Dominion
Empire-builders	Erbauer des Empire
interior [ɪn'tɪərɪə]	das Innere
to penetrate	eindringen
explorer	Forschungsreisende(r)
missionary	Missionar/in
Crown Colony	Kronkolonie
protectorate [prə'tektərət]	Schutzgebiet, Protektorat
to retain	zurückbehalten
vestige ['vestɪdʒ]	Spur, Überbleibsel
dependency	abhängiges Gebiet
Gibraltar [dʒɪ'brɔ:ltə]	Gibraltar (Kronkolonie)
association [əˌsəʊsɪ'eɪʃn]	Vereinigung, Staatenbund
rank	Stellung, Status
allegiance to [ə'li:dʒəns]	Treue gegenüber

association [əˌsəʊsɪ'eɪʃn]	Vereinigung, Staatenbund
decolonization	Abschaffung des Kolonialismus
Asia ['eɪʃə]	Asien
the Caribbean [ˌkærɪ'bi:ən]	Karibik
to attain	erreichen, erlangen
diversity [daɪ'vɜ:sɪtɪ]	Vielfalt
Barbados [bɑ:'beɪdəʊz]	Barbados (Insel in der Karibik)
multi-racial [ˌmʌltɪ'reɪʃl]	vielrassig
faith	Glauben, *hier:* Religion
head	*hier:* Oberhaupt

The relationships between members are based on economic co-operation, their main link. Since 1962 Britain has given financial aid (low-interest loans) especially to Third-World members to promote their industrial and agricultural production. Britain also fostered Commonwealth trade by means of preferential tariffs on imports, but its economic interest has shifted to European markets since it joined the European Community (EC) in 1973. In consequence, some Commonwealth countries have meanwhile become EC associates with reduced-duty access to the EC.

relationship	Beziehungen, Verhältnis
link	Verbindung, Bindeglied
aid	Hilfe
low-interest	Niedrigzins-
loan	Anleihe
to promote	fördern
to foster	begünstigen, fördern
preferential [ˌprefəˈrenʃl]	Vorzugs-
tariff	Zoll
to shift	(sich) verlagern
European Community (EC)	Europäische Gemeinschaft
associate [əˈsəʊʃɪət]	außerordentliches Mitglied
duty	*hier:* Zoll
access	Zugang

A Europe without frontiers

GB's troubled years in Europe

Unity – an elusive goal?

A United States of Europe?

The European Community (EC)

Basic information:

The EC – or EEC (European Economic Community) or Common Market as it is also called in Britain – was established in 1957 in the Treaty of Rome. There were originally 6 member states. Britain joined the EC in 1973.

It is a market catering for the needs of more than 330 million people or consumers. Most of the tariffs have already been abolished in trade between the individual Common Market members, but there are still barriers in the form of regulations and internal taxes and also cross-border controls between the different member states.

frontier ['frʌnˌtɪə]	Grenze
elusive [ɪ'lu:sɪv]	schwer zu erreichen

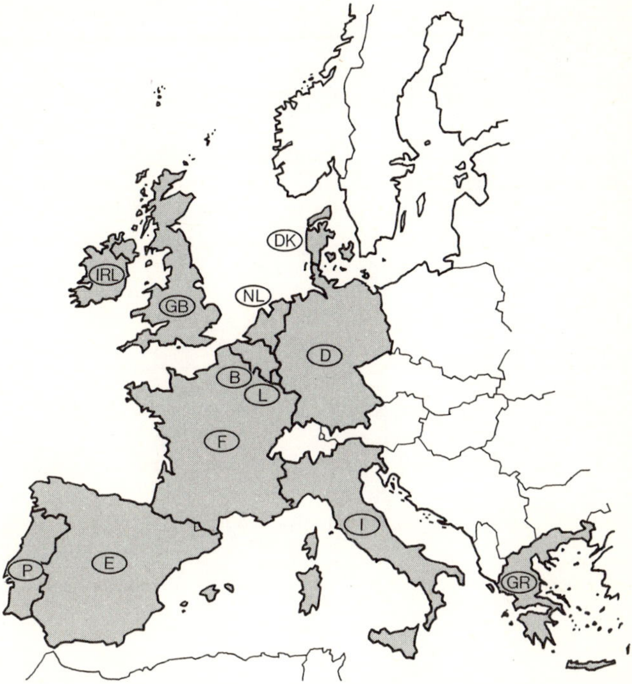

EC (European Community)	die Europäische Gemeinschaft (EG)
Common Market	der Gemeinsame Markt
treaty	Vertrag
member state	Mitgliedsland
to cater for	*hier:* befriedigen
consumer	Verbraucher/in
tariff	Zoll
to abolish [ə'bɒlɪʃ]	abschaffen
barrier ['bærɪə]	Schranke
regulation	Regelung
internal	Binnen-
tax	Steuer
cross-border control	Grenzkontrolle

Aims of the EC:

1. the establishment of a tariff-free internal market, a single European market/ trading bloc,
2. the creation of an economic and monetary union and a liberalization of capital transfer,
3. the introduction of a single currency and a European Central Bank,
4. the provision of more freedom for the citizens of the Community in a Europe in which they can work, study and travel without hindrance,
5. financial aid for Europe's poorest regions,
6. industrial and technological development so that Europe can compete with the USA and Japan, for example in high-tech fields,
7. Europe's economic, social and political integration with a view to creating a United States of Europe.

General problems:

1. Full integration, e.g. the political union of so many different European states, is very difficult to achieve.
2. The farm subsidies: storage costs of surplus food are too high.
3. Under the present system the VAT and excise duties charged on wine, tobacco and other goods vary widely: 'approximation' and harmonization are necessary.
4. The removal of border controls could make life easier for illegal immigrants, drug dealers or terrorists.

Problems of Britain in the EC:

Integrating Britain into the EC fully is difficult because of the distrust of many British politicians of being governed by institutions on the Continent (in Brussels or Strasbourg).

There has been opposition to membership of the Common Market from the beginning. But a withdrawal is no longer a realistic option for the British. The majority of people want Britain to remain a member of the Common Market, but many are against

- the creation of a European Central Bank,
- an increase in worker participation / co-determination in companies,
- the transference of national sovereignty and decision-making from the national parliament in Westminister to EC institutions,
- excessive bureaucracy, centralization and over-regulation.

trading bloc	Handelsblock
monetary ['mʌnɪtərɪ]	Geld-, Währungs-
capital transfer ['trænsfɜː]	Kapitalfluß, Kapitaltransfer
currency	Währung
citizen	Bürger/in
hindrance	Behinderung
aid	Hilfe
to compete with	konkurrieren mit
high-tech [–tek]	hochtechnologisch
integration	Eingliederung, Integration
subsidies ['sʌbsɪdiːz]	Subventionen
storage ['stɔːrɪdʒ]	Lagerung
surplus ['sɜːpləs]	Überschuß, überschüssig
VAT (value added tax)	Mehrwertsteuer
excise ['eksaɪz] **duties**	Verbrauchssteuern
approximation [əˌprɒksɪ'meɪʃən]	Annäherung, Angleichung
harmonization	Abstimmung aufeinander
removal	Beseitigung
immigrant	Einwanderer
drug dealer	Drogenhändler
politician [ˌpɒlɪ'tɪʃən]	Politiker/in
withdrawal [wɪð'drɔːəl]	Rückzug, Ausstieg
option	*hier:* Alternative
worker participation/co-determination	Mitbestimmung
transference ['trænsfərəns]	Übertragung
sovereignty ['sɒvrəntɪ]	Landeshoheit
excessive	übermäßig
bureaucracy [bjʊə'rɒkrəsɪ]	Bürokratie
over-regulation	zu viele u. strenge Vorschriften, übertriebene Regulierung

In their view the creation of a United States of Europe, based on the model provided by the United States of America, is an unattainable goal because, among other things, the cultures and languages of the countries involved are too different. They do not object to the development of a more powerful trading bloc and the extension of free trade between the EC states, but prefer co-operation between sovereign states to a merging of national identities.

unattainable	unerreichbar
goal	Ziel
extension	Erweiterung
to merge [mɜ:dʒ]	verschmelzen

Billion Dollar Budget Deficit in the USA

Inflation Rate in GB at 7.5 per cent, Unemployment Rate near 2million

Trade Surplus

Third World Debt Tragedy

The Economy

Basic information:

Most of the countries in the world belonged until recently to one of the two economic systems: the free-enterprise system (including most of the Western world, Australia, Japan etc.) and the planned-economy system of state capitalism in the Eastern-bloc countries. But more and more countries are now trying to achieve a balance between private enterprise and state intervention / regulation in their national economies.

Politicians and economic experts are responsible for the financial and economic well-being of their countries. They may be Members of Parliament (MPs) or Cabinet members like the Chancellor of the Exchequer (GB) or the U.S. Treasury Secretary (i.e. the finance ministers of their countries).

An important role is also played by other state institutions like the Bank of England or the Fed(eral Reserve Board/System) in the USA (the central banks of their countries), which try to keep the world's main currency, the US dollar, and the other important currencies (the Deutschmark, the Japanese yen, the pound sterling = £) stable.

Most countries are afraid of a lack of monetary stability, of rising price levels resulting in a higher inflation rate. Almost every country's currency loses some of its value and purchasing power every year.

billion *(AE)*	Milliarde
budget ['bʌdʒət]	Haushalt
inflation rate	Inflationsrate
trade surplus ['sɜ:pləs]	Handelsüberschuß
debt(s) [det]	Schulden

free enterprise	freie Marktwirtschaft
planned economy	Planwirtschaft
state capitalism	Staatskapitalismus
Eastern-bloc country	Ostblockland
intervention	Eingreifen, Intervention
Parliament ['pɑ:ləmənt]	Parlament
Cabinet	Kabinett (die Minister in der Regierung)
Chancellor of the Exchequer [ɪks'tʃekə] *(BE)*	Schatzkanzler/in
Treasury ['treʒərɪ] **Secretary** *(AE)*	Finanzminister/in
central bank	Zentralbank (z. B. Deutsche Bundesbank)
currency ['kʌrənsɪ]	Währung
stable	stabil
monetary ['mʌnɪtərɪ]	finanziell, Geld-
level	Niveau
purchasing ['pɜ:tʃəsɪŋ] **power**	Kaufkraft

The inflation rate may be at a low level, may rise at a moderate pace or may be soaring. A higher inflation rate normally leads to higher pay settlements, to more consumer spending, to higher prices and thus to an even higher inflation rate: economists speak of a wage and price spiral.

Prices, for example consumer (food) prices, energy (fuel oil) and commodity (such as copper) prices, or those of manufactured goods, can be stable, go up by some per cent, go down or even plummet.

Features of a successful economic policy:

1. steady economic growth (increase in industrial output / production; many factories or companies, for example, already run three shifts), an annual rise in the gross national product (GNP),
2. stability of prices (a low rate of inflation),
3. full employment (or at least a low unemployment rate),
4. both public and private sectors make profits/are profitable and can cut costs thanks to moderate pay settlements, automation, rationalization etc. resulting in a growth in productivity,
5. trade barriers and tariffs fall, free trade and competitiveness increase and new markets are created worldwide,
6. more money is spent on the country's social security system and welfare programmes (e.g. retirement benefits and disability payments, more money for the US Medicaid programme),
7. a balance is maintained between supply and demand.

Methods of stimulating growth:

1. Deficit spending increases budget deficits but makes more money available for the creation of new jobs.
2. Taxes can be reduced to lower production costs, to ease labour cost pressures and to create new incentives for private companies (a measure typical of the supply-side economics in the USA and GB in the 1980s).

moderate ['mɒdərət]	gemäßigt
to soar [sɔː]	in die Höhe schnellen
pay settlement	Lohnabschluß
consumer spending	Verbraucher-, Konsumausgaben
wage and price spiral ['spaɪərəl]	Lohn- und Preisspirale
fuel oil	Heizöl
commodity [kə'mɒdətɪ]	Ware
copper	Kupfer
manufactured [ˌmænjʊ'fæktʃəd] **goods**	Fertigwaren
to plummet	fallen, stürzen
policy	Politik, politische Linie
output	Ausstoß, Produktion
shift	Schicht
gross national product [grəʊs]	Bruttosozialprodukt
automation	Automatisierung
rationalization ['ræʃnəlaɪ'zeɪʃn]	Rationalisierung
productivity	Produktivität
trade barrier	Handelsschranke
tariff	Zoll
competitiveness [kəm'petətɪvnɪs]	Wettbewerbsfähigkeit
competitor	Mitbewerber/in, Konkurrent/in
social security	Sozialversicherung, -hilfe
welfare programme	Sozialprogramm
retirement benefits	Ruhestandszahlungen, Renten
disability	Invalidität, Arbeitsunfähigkeit
Medicaid *(US)*	Gesundheitsfürsorge (USA) für Bedürftige
supply and demand	Angebot und Nachfrage
to stimulate	beleben, ankurbeln
deficit spending	Defizitfinanzierung
to ease	*hier:* verringern
labour costs	Lohnkosten
incentive	Anreiz
supply-side economics	angebotsorientierte Wirtschaftspolitik

3. If there is no tight monetary control, a greater money supply can lower interest rates, so that investment and domestic consumption are stimulated.

General problems:

1. Periods of economic growth and stability alternating with periods of economic decline and recession,
2. bankruptcy of some national economies,
3. owing to the slowness of industry to innovate and a general reluctance to invest and to abandon traditional industries and work practices, some businesses are no longer competitive,
4. labour disputes between the two sides of industry (employers / management – employees / trade unions) may lead to lockouts and strikes.
5. the manufacturing sector is too small or the agricultural sector too inefficient, especially in Third-World countries,
6. low prices for the country's export commodities and natural resources (such as coffee, sugar, crude oil or copper),
7. big companies/corporations/multinationals are able to control the markets (and price levels) worldwide; anti-trust laws have been introduced to try to prevent them from becoming too powerful and from securing a monopoly.

Problems of industrialized countries:

Industrialized countries, as compared with developing countries, have strong national economies and currencies. Some, because the export side of their balance of payments is high, have huge trade surpluses. Production costs are high, but productivity has also increased and their sophisticated high-tech products sell well on the world market.

Automation and rationalization have led to a relatively high rate of unemployment in the labour-intensive industries like coal-mining and shipbuilding, but many new jobs have been created in the new service industries like information technology, tourism and leisure.

tight	*hier:* streng
interest rate	Zinssatz
investment	Investition
domestic	inländisch

to alternate	wechseln
recession	Konjunkturrückgang, Rezession
bankruptcy ['bæŋkrəptsɪ]	Bankrott, Konkurs
to innovate	Neuerungen vornehmen
reluctance	Widerstreben, Abneigung
to abandon [ə'bændən]	*hier:* aufgeben
competitive [kəm'petətɪv]	konkurrenzfähig
dispute	Streit, Auseinandersetzung
employer	Arbeitgeber/in
employee [ˌemplɔɪ'i:]	Angestellte(r), Arbeiter/in
trade union	Gewerkschaft
lockout	Aussperrung
strike	Streik
manufacturing sector	der produzierende (Industrie-) Sektor
natural resources [rɪ'sɔ:sɪz]	Bodenschätze
crude oil	Rohöl
multinational	internationale Weltfirma, Multi
to control	beherrschen
anti-trust laws	Kartellgesetze
monopoly [mə'nɒpəlɪ]	Monopol

industrialized country	Industrieland
developing country	Entwicklungsland
balance of payments	Zahlungsbilanz
trade surplus	Exportüberschuß
sophisticated [sə'fɪstɪˌkeɪtɪd]	raffiniert, hochentwickelt
labour-intensive [-ɪn'tensɪv]	arbeitsintensiv
service industries	Dienstleistungsbetriebe
information technology	Informationstechnik
leisure ['leʒə] **industry**	Freizeitindustrie

Problems of developing countries:

Their imports exceed their exports, they suffer from huge current-account deficits, from export and import imbalances and trade barriers.
Industrialized countries prevent some Third-World products from getting access to their markets by imposing protective tariffs.
Most Third-World countries have huge debts, owing the international banks and other creditors billions of dollars. Their foreign exchange reserves are so depleted that some cannot even pay the interest rates on the loans. Their rural export earnings cannot cover the costs of the import of necessary goods like machines or fuel products. Some countries dependent on the export of one product only (coffee, bananas or copper, for example) are trying to diversify their exports.
Curbing inflation and reducing huge deficits and unemployment are other top priorities in stabilizing an ailing economy.

current-account deficit	Leistungsbilanzdefizit
protective tariffs	Schutzzölle
debt(s) [det]	Schuld(en)
to owe	schulden
creditor	Gläubiger/in
foreign exchange	*hier:* Devisen
to deplete	erschöpfen
loan	Darlehen, Kredit
rural	*hier:* landwirtschaftlich
earnings	Gewinne
to diversify [daɪ'vɜ:sɪfaɪ]	verschiedenartig gestalten
to curb	eindämmen
top priority [praɪ'ɒrətɪ]	*hier:* Schwerpunkt
ailing	leidend, dahinsiechend

The Welfare State and Social Security

Social Welfare in Britain

Although Britain had already had compulsory health and unemployment insurance and non-contributory old-age pensions since the early 20th century, the term 'social security' first appeared in an official context in 1944. The welfare state of today can be traced back to the Beveridge Report of 1942, in which the Liberal MP Lord Beveridge supplied a strategy for combating the various social ills and for taking care of everyone in need. Thus social security was to be comprehensive: all citizens living in want were to be guaranteed a minimum income, government subsidies were to help solve the problems of the housing shortage and the squalor of the slums, nobody able and willing to work was to be condemned to idleness, the sick were to be cared for by a national health service and all children were to receive an appropriate education.

Guided by the ideas outlined in this report, the Labour government passed a series of acts between 1945 and 1951. This legislation was designed to cover the following: sickness, industrial injury, unemployment, the death of the bread-winner (i. e. provision for widows and orphans), family allowances, medical attention and loss of income through retirement.

Some examples of state benefits are unemployment benefits, supplementary benefits (e. g. Family Insurance Income Supplement), allowances for children, benefits for the elderly and disabled, old-age pensions and retirement benefits, housing benefits and disability pensions.

The welfare state in Britain includes the so-called 'personal services' (provided by local authorities and charities, which take personal care of children, the elderly and the disabled), the National Health Service (NHS) and the social security services. The NHS used to make free hospital and other medical treatment available to all, whereas those who are better off must now pay a small contribution. However, there are also a number of private hospitals, doctors and dentists catering for patients who desire prompter, and sometimes better, service.

compulsory [kəm'pʌlsərɪ]	Pflicht-
insurance	Versicherung
non-contributory [-kən'trɪbjʊtərɪ]	nicht beitragspflichtig
pension	Rente
to supply	bereitstellen, liefern
to combat ['kɔmbæt]	bekämpfen
ill *n*	*hier:* Mißstand
comprehensive	(all-) umfassend
want	Not
subsidies *pl* ['sʌbsɪdi:z]	Subventionen
squalor ['skwɒlə]	Schmutz, Elend
to condemn	verurteilen
idleness	Beschäftigungslosigkeit
appropriate	angemessen
series ['sɪəri:z]	Reihe
to cover	*hier:* abdecken
industrial injury	Arbeits-, Betriebsunfall
provision	*hier:* Versorgungsleistung
orphan	Waise
allowance	Unterstützung, Beihilfe
attention	*hier:* Fürsorge, Pflege
retirement	Ruhestand, Pension
benefits	Rente, Unterstützung
supplementary benefits	Sozialhilfe
the elderly	die Alten, Senioren
disabled	erwerbsunfähig, behindert, invalide
disability pension	Invalidenrente
charity	Wohlfahrtseinrichtung
treatment	Behandlung
contribution	Beitrag
to cater for	sorgen für

Social Welfare in the US

The expression 'social security' was coined in the US, although Americans had traditionally regarded care of the poor and needy as the responsibility not of the state but of charitable institutions, churches etc. However, the widespread poverty and suffering following the Great Depression of 1929 made it clear that the countless innocent victims could be helped only if the state was willing to shoulder the task of providing them with the essentials. An act was therefore passed in 1935, in which the term 'social security' first officially appeared and in which the state committed itself to providing the following: old-age, survivor's and unemployment insurance, maternal and child welfare and public assistance for the poor. In the Social Security Act of 1965 benefits were increased and 'Medicare', a health scheme providing medical care for old people, was introduced.

Although the US does not have a national health scheme comparable to the NHS in Britain, care for Americans too poor to meet their medical expenses is provided by 'Medicaid'. While the majority of Americans have health insurance that is paid for by their employers or bought from an insurance company, there are still millions of people without their own private health insurance and thus dependent on the government.

Other social security programmes provide and finance unemployment benefits, food stamps, heating assistance, day care for children, sick leave etc. Nowadays survival without the safety net of social security would be difficult, in some cases even impossible, for innumerable Americans.

to coin	prägen
charitable	wohltätig, karitativ
poverty	Armut
the Great Depression	Weltwirtschaftskrise
victim	Opfer, Betroffene(r)
to shoulder	auf sich nehmen
the essentials	das Lebensnotwendige
to commit oneself	sich verpflichten
maternal and child welfare	Fürsorge für Mutter und Kind
Medicare *(US)*	Gesundheitsfürsorge für Ältere
scheme [ski:m]	Plan
comparable ['kɒmpərəbl]	vergleichbar
Medicaid *(US)*	Gesundheitsprogramm für Bedürftige
employer	Arbeitgeber/in
insurance company	Versicherungsgesellschaft
food stamp	Lebensmittelbon, -gutschein
day care	Tagesbetreuung
sick leave	bezahlter Urlaub im Krankheitsfall
safety net	Sicherheitsnetz

Feminists' frustration
in a male-dominated society

Female farmworkers may
go to court over equal pay

Women's continued struggle for equality

Women in Society

Basic information:

Women's Lib, the Women's Liberation Movement, emerged in the 1960s, although the liberation and emancipation of women in society had actually started in the 19th century. At that time women were not allowed to vote, and female suffrage, introduced in Britain as late as 1928, brought only political but not full social equality.

Fortunately, the days of second-class citizenship for women are largely over and the liberation of women both in the private and in the public sphere is making good progress:

1. Laws have been passed to outlaw sexual discrimination.
2. The number of working women is increasing: in developed countries women make up 30 to 50 per cent of the workforce (and even more in Eastern Europe).
3. More and more women now have access to and find self-realization in careers in previously male-dominated fields, such as in business, medicine, data processing and skilled manual work.

feminist	Frauenrechtler/in, Feminist/in
male-dominated	von Männern beherrscht
female	weiblich
to go to court	vor Gericht gehen
equality [ɪ'kwɔlətɪ]	Gleichheit

Women's Lib	Frauenemanzipationsbewegung
to emerge	entstehen
emancipation	Befreiung, Emanzipation
female suffrage ['sʌfrɪdʒ]	Stimmrecht für Frauen
citizenship	Staatsbürgerschaft
to outlaw	verbieten
discrimination	Benachteiligung, Diskriminierung
workforce	Arbeitnehmerschaft, Belegschaft
self-realization	Selbstverwirklichung
data ['deɪtə] **processing**	Datenverarbeitung
skilled	gelernt, qualifiziert
manual work	(Hand-)Arbeit

4. Women's centres/shelters, in which women in distress can take refuge, have been set up.
5. Birth-control, contraception and abortion are no longer taboo words or subjects.
6. Many books on feminist issues have been published.
7. A shift in traditional female/male roles is taking place: it is becoming more and more common for wives and husbands to divide the household tasks fairly between them, although many working women still bear the brunt of the domestic burden.

Feminists argue:

1. After decades of 'emancipation' and 'liberation' only little has changed for the majority of women: there is still widespread, sometimes even overt, discrimination and prejudice against working women; equal pay for equal work is guaranteed by law, but is not always the practice.
2. There is only slow progress in the struggle for equal job opportunities: large numbers of women are employed in low-grade work, particularly in the service sector and the textile industry; even well-qualified women have less chance than men of becoming bank managers or top executives.
3. Life is harder for many women than it used to be because many have to go out to work to supplement the family's income as well as running the household: such a 'double burden' is a great strain on the women and on family life.
4 In cases of redundancy it is often the unskilled women with their part-time jobs that are sacked first.
5 Women often retire at an earlier age than men: women's pensions are therefore lower.

women's centre/shelter	Frauenhaus
refuge ['refju:dʒ]	Zuflucht
birth-control	Geburtenkontrolle
contraception	Empfängnisverhütung
abortion [ə'bɔ:ʃn]	Abtreibung
issue ['ɪʃju:]	Streitfrage, Problem
shift	Verschiebung, Verlagerung
to bear the brunt	die Hauptlast tragen
overt ['əʊvɜ:t]	offen
prejudice ['predʒʊdɪs]	Vorurteil
equal job opportunities	Chancengleichheit am Arbeitsplatz
service sector	Dienstleistungssektor
top executive [ɪg'zekjʊtɪv]	leitender(r) Angestellte(r), Geschäftsführer/in
to supplement ['sʌplɪment]	ergänzen
to run the household	den Haushalt führen
double burden	Doppelbelastung
strain (on)	Belastung (für)
redundancy [rɪ'dʌndənsɪ]	Arbeitslosigkeit
to sack	entlassen, 'feuern'
to retire	*hier:* in Rente gehen

The melting pot that does not work

New curbs on immigrants urged

Giving immigrants the right to be different

Is racism on the rise?

Racial Problems: Immigrants in Great Britain

Basic information:

Most European countries have large immigrant populations: in Germany they are mainly from Turkey, in France from North Africa and in Britain from Asia and the West Indies. There are now more than 2 million immigrants in the United Kingdom (about 4 per cent of the population).

Being citizens of Commonwealth countries, they immigrated into Britain legally as British subjects. One of the big waves of immigration occurred in the 1940s and 1950s, after the Second World War, when hundreds of thousands of coloured people went to Britain.

These immigrants often provided cheap labour for industry. They regarded themselves as guest workers who wanted to earn money, send it home to their families and return to their native countries after amassing enough capital to build their own houses, set up their own businesses, open shops etc. Most of them, however, though often disillusioned with Britain, decided to settle there.

melting pot	Schmelztiegel
curbs *(pl)*	*hier:* strengere Einwanderungsbestimmungen
to urge	drängen auf
racism	Rassismus

immigrant	Einwanderer
citizen	Bürger/in
to immigrate	einwandern
subject	Untertan/in
wave	Welle
immigration	Einwanderung
coloured	farbig
to provide	*hier:* sorgen für, bereitstellen
cheap labour	billige Arbeitskräfte
guest worker	Gastarbeiter/in
native	Heimat-
to amass [ə'mæs]	anhäufen
disillusioned [ˌdɪsɪ'lu:ʒnd] **with**	enttäuscht von

Many coloured people living in Britain today are second- or third-generation immigrants, which means that their parents or grandparents were immigrants (about 40 per cent of all coloured people in Britain were born there). Being trapped between two cultures and not really belonging to either, they often feel alienated from society and uncertain about their own identity.

Being for the most part unskilled workers, they are employed in various branches of industry (e.g. the textile industry) and in the service sector, where they work as bus-drivers, dustmen, street sweepers etc. Of course, not all of them are engaged in menial tasks or manual labour. A considerable number, especially Indians and Pakistanis, work as small businessmen, shopkeepers, teachers and doctors.

Because of unemployment and other social problems, the British government has curbed the influx of immigrants into the country. Entry requirements have been tightened and stricter laws on immigration introduced. Immigrants who have somehow managed to enter Britain illegally face deportation or forced repatriation if caught.

Some reasons for racial tensions:

1. Whites and immigrants compete for scarce jobs.
2. Substandard housing is often the only kind available to immigrants, many of whom live in run-down council estates and tower blocks in inner-city areas.
3. Second- or third-generation immigrants are more demanding and self-assertive and less willing to subordinate themselves to the whites.
4. Racial abuse by whites provokes similar hostile reactions and retaliation on the part of the immigrants.

Possible solutions:

1. Guaranteeing the allocation of funds for improving and expanding social services (e.g. social centres), for job creation and job training,
2. setting up community relations councils,
3. investing in better housing,
4. giving the immigrants the right to vote,
5. employing and training more coloured police officers in order to reduce racial tension, improve community relations and ensure harmony and peaceful co-existence in troubled neighbourhoods.

to be trapped	*hier:* in der Falle sitzen
to alienate ['eɪljəneɪt]	entfremden
unskilled	ungelernt
textile	Textil-
service sector	Dienstleistungssektor
menial ['mi:njəl]	niedrig
influx ['ɪnflʌks]	Zustrom
requirement	Bedingung, Voraussetzung
to tighten	verschärfen
deportation	Ausweisung, Deportation
repatriation [ˌri:pætrɪ'eɪʃn]	Rückführung in die Heimat
to compete for	in Wettstreit treten um
housing	*hier:* Häuser
run-down	heruntergekommen
council estate [ɪ'steɪt]	Siedlung mit Sozialwohnungen
self-assertive [-ə'sɜ:tɪv]	selbstbewußt, durchsetzungsfähig
to subordinate o.s. to [sə'bɔ:dɪneɪt]	sich unterordnen
abuse [ə'bju:s]	Beschimpfung, Beleidigung
retaliation [rɪˌtælɪ'eɪʃn]	Vergeltung
allocation	Zuweisung
funds	Geldmittel
job creation	Schaffung von Arbeitsplätzen
job training	Berufsausbildung
community relations council	Beirat/Komitee zur Pflege der nachbarschaftl. Beziehungen
right to vote	Stimmrecht
co-existence [kəʊɪg'zɪstəns]	Zusammenleben, Koexistenz
neighbourhood	Viertel, Wohngegend

The dream of Martin Luther King is blurred by apathy and drugs

The gap between better-off and poor blacks grows wider

Racial Problems: Blacks in the USA

Basic information:

There are about 28 million blacks in the USA, roughly twelve per cent of the population. The majority are descendants of slaves 'imported' from Africa to work on the plantations in the South of the USA. President Lincoln's Emancipation Proclamation of 1863 expressed the government's intention of putting an end to slavery, which was subsequently abolished in 1865 after the Civil War. Many former slaves moved north, east and west to the big cities in search of work, becoming the first blacks to live in urban ghettos.

Although government efforts to fight segregation and prevent discrimination against blacks were at a standstill for decades, some progress was made in certain areas. It was not until the 1960s, however, that black leaders like Martin Luther King were able to mobilize large sections of

blurred	*hier:* undeutlich, nebelhaft, verwischt
apathy ['æpəθɪ]	Teilnahmslosigkeit, Apathie
gap	Kluft, Unterschied

descendant [dɪ'sendənt]	Nachkomme
plantation	Plantage
Emancipation Proclamation	Verkündung der Sklavenbefreiung
slavery	Sklaverei
to abolish [ə'bɒlɪʃ]	abschaffen
Civil War	nordamerikanischer Bürgerkrieg (1861–65)
urban ghetto	städtisches Ghetto
segregation	(Rassen)Trennung
discrimination against	Benachteiligung von

both the black and white population and launch the Civil Rights Movement. Thanks to the public sympathy for and interest in the black cause aroused by the non-violent marches, demonstrations and protests, legislative measures became inevitable: the Civil Rights Act of 1964 was passed, which aimed at racial desegregation by granting blacks equality in all political and social fields, including the right to vote.

The lot of American blacks has improved considerably over the last few decades. Better-off blacks have escaped from the decaying and crime-ridden city centres to the suburbs, where they feel more secure than in their old neighbourhoods. Poor blacks, however, are trapped in their urban ghettos, where poverty, violence, drug trafficking and despair are endemic.

Positive changes:

1. Race is no longer the issue it was before and during the 1950s and 1960s, when racial prejudice and pejorative terms for blacks were common. There is no longer firm and widespread belief in the notions of black inferiority and white superiority.
2. Intermarriage has gained widespread acceptance.
3. A black middle class has emerged, and black millionaires, mayors and even aspiring presidential candidates are no longer unusual.
4. Racism is on the decline: the racial strife of the sixties, a decade marked by clashes between blacks and their white supporters on the one side and racist sheriffs and Klansmen on the other, is now largely a thing of the past, as is the role played by the Ku-Klux-Klan in Southern politics.
5. Besides continuing to play a prominent role in the entertainment sector, blacks have also come to dominate certain areas of sport, e.g. boxing, basketball, track and field etc.
6. As a result of the integration of increasing numbers of middle-class blacks into formerly ‘white’ residential areas, there are now many racially mixed suburban communities.
7. Segregation no longer exists in public schools and it has also vanished in playgrounds, restaurants, hotels and other public establishments and facilities; blacks can be said to enjoy far greater racial equality and to be confronted with fewer racial barriers than in the past.

Civil Rights Movement	Bürgerrechtsbewegung
non-violent	gewaltlos
legislative ['ledʒɪslətɪv]	gesetzgebend, legislativ
act	Gesetz
desegregation	Aufhebung der Rassentrennung
equality [iːˈkwɒlətɪ]	Gleichheit
lot	Schicksal, Los
to decay [dɪˈkeɪ]	verfallen
crime-ridden	von Verbrechen heimgesucht
suburb [ˈsʌbɜːb]	Vorort
neighbourhood	Viertel, Wohngegend
to be trapped	*hier:* gefangen sein
drug trafficking	Drogenhandel
endemic [enˈdemɪk]	heimisch, vorherrschend

issue [ˈɪʃjuː]	Problem, Kernfrage, Streitfrage
racial prejudice [ˈpredʒʊdɪs]	Rassenvorurteil
pejorative [pɪˈdʒɒrətɪv]	abschätzig
notion	Ansicht
inferiority [ɪnˌfɪərɪˈɒrətɪ]	Unterlegenheit, Minderwertigkeit
superiority [suːˌpɪərɪˈɒrətɪ]	Überlegenheit
intermarriage [ˌɪntəˈmærɪdʒ]	Mischehe
mayor [meə]	Bürgermeister/in
racism	Rassismus
strife	Kampf
racist/a racist	rassistisch, ein Rassist
Klansman	Mitglied des Ku-Klux-Klan
Ku-Klux-Klan [ˌkjuːklʌksˈklæn]	rassistischer Geheimbund in den USA
track and field	Leichtathletik
integration	Eingliederung, Integration
residential area	Wohnviertel

facilities	Einrichtungen
to be confronted with …	auf … stoßen, … gegenüberstehen
barrier [ˈbærɪə]	Schranke

Problems still facing the blacks:

1. Although overt discrimination has fortunately largely disappeared in all spheres of life – politics, education, law, housing, recreation, sports, religion etc. – hidden discrimination against blacks still exists. The brutal segregation of earlier decades has been replaced by more subtle forms of discrimination.
2. Race relations have improved only superficially and to a limited extent. Black and white colleagues who mingle amicably at work tend to lead separate social lives after working hours. Even liberal whites who express enthusiasm for integration in theory are not always keen to promote it in practice by mixing socially with blacks.
3. Despite the advances made in politics at a local level, blacks remain under-represented at the state and federal level, especially in Congress and the Administration.
4. The most urgent problem is undeniably that of the 'underclass'. There is now great disparity in income and social standing between successful middle-class blacks and the growing underclass. Most members of the latter live in inner-city ghettos, hotbeds of drug trafficking and crime and the scene of gang warfare between rival black or Hispanic groups. Nearly half of these underclass blacks live below the poverty line and are chronically dependent on welfare, food stamps and Medicaid benefits.

   The unemployment rate of blacks is well above average. About one third of black teenagers drop out of high school. More than half of all black families are headed by one parent only. The infant mortality rate among blacks is double that of whites. Remedies are urgently needed if the underclass is not to become alienated from the rest of American society, whose belief in the work ethic and the possibility of upward mobility remains intact.

overt ['əʊvɜ:t]	offen, öffentlich
housing	Wohnverhältnisse
recreation [ˌrekrɪ'eɪʃən]	*hier:* Freizeit, Freizeitbeschäftigung
subtle ['sʌtl]	fein, subtil
race relations	Rassenbeziehungen
superficial [ˌsu:pə'fɪʃl]	oberflächlich
to mingle	sich mischen
amicable ['æmɪkəbl]	freundlich
separate ['seprət]	getrennt
enthusiasm [ɪn'θju:zɪæzəm]	Begeisterung
to mix with	(gesellschaftlich) verkehren mit
under-represented	unterrepräsentiert
Congress	Kongreß
Administration *(AE)*	Regierung
disparity	Ungleichheit, Unterschied
social standing	gesellschaftliche Stellung
hotbed	Brutstätte
gang warfare	Bandenkriege
Hispanic [hɪ'spænɪk]	US-Bürger/in spanischer Kultur
poverty line	Armutsgrenze
welfare	Wohlfahrt
food stamp	Lebensmittelgutschein
Medicaid	Gesundheitsfürsorge für Bedürftige
benefits	Beihilfe, Unterstützung
to drop out	(die Schule) abbrechen
infant mortality rate	Säuglingssterblichkeit
remedy	Abhilfe
to alienate ['eɪljəneɪt]	entfremden
work ethic	Arbeitsmoral
upward mobility	sozialer Aufstieg

Racial Problems: South Africa

Basic information:

South Africa, a 'white' state in southern Africa, is bordered by 'black' neighbours: Namibia, Zimbabwe, Mozambique etc. It is inhabited by about 30 million blacks (including people of mixed race known as Coloureds), by 5 million whites (most of whom are descendants of settlers from Britain or the Netherlands) and by one million Indians. The Dutch settlers, who fought and lost a war against the British at the turn of this century, were called Boers. They introduced 'Afrikaans', the second official language besides English, into the country and their descendants are now called 'Afrikaner'.

South Africa is the richest country in Africa, which makes it very different from the developing countries typical of that continent. Its huge mining and industrial sectors have efficiently exploited its enormous and valuable mineral resources such as gold, diamonds, platinum and uranium.

The economy is basically divided into two parts: big multinational companies, banks and white management and ownership of the mining industries on the one hand and black labour in the mines and the service sector on the other. The economy, though run by whites, is dependent on cheap black labour. However, while most blacks remain economically disadvantaged, a middle class of well-educated and well-qualified blacks is slowly growing.

For decades political power was in the hands of the white minority. Most blacks, with no right to vote except in local elections, felt oppressed by the white minority regime and rejected the policy of apartheid, the separate development of black and white.

In the early 1990s the ruling National Party abolished the apartheid laws and took decisive steps towards social and racial integration and political power-sharing. Today many whites fear the reprisals, political chaos, economic collapse and expulsion that might occur under black majority rule.

To prevent social unrest and destabilization, the important opposition groups such as the ANC (African National Congress) were banned for a long time. Most blacks now try to avoid violence and pursue peaceful methods, but some press for the use of violence against whites and black rival groups. There is a great need for reconciliation between the people on both sides of the colour bar.

Coloureds	Farbige
descendant	Nachkomme
Boer ['bəʊə]	Bure (Nachfahre holländischer Einwanderer)
mining sector	Bergbausektor
to exploit	ausbeuten
mineral resources [rɪ'sɔ:sɪz]	Bodenschätze
multinational company	multinationaler Konzern, 'Multi'
service sector	Dienstleistungssektor
cheap labour	billige Arbeitskräfte
disadvantaged	benachteiligt
right to vote	Stimmrecht
regime [reɪ'ʒi:m]	Regime
to reject	ablehnen
apartheid [ə'pɑ:theɪt]	Apartheid (System der Rassentrennung in Südafrika)
separate ['seprət]	getrennt
to abolish [ə'bɒlɪʃ]	abschaffen
integration	Eingliederung, Integration
power-sharing	Teilung der Macht
reprisals [rɪ'praɪzlz]	Vergeltungsmaßnahmen
collapse	Zusammenbruch
expulsion	Vertreibung
social unrest	soziale Unruhen
destabilization	Verunsicherung, Destabilisierung
to ban	verbieten
to pursue [pə'sju:]	nachgehen, verfolgen
to press for	drängen auf, fordern
reconciliation [ˌrekənsɪlɪ'eɪʃn]	Versöhnung
colour bar	Rassenschranke

The system of apartheid:

Apartheid meant racial segregation, separation of the black and white races. Each race was to develop separately. One of the most important reasons why most blacks rejected apartheid was that it involved the classification of South Africans according to racial criteria, the legal practice of placing them in racial categories (Population Registration Act).

Since apartheid has been abolished, many changes have taken place, for example:

- interracial marriage is no longer forbidden by law
- blacks are no longer obliged to occupy different sections on buses, in restaurants, cinemas, on beaches, park benches etc.
- equal pay for equal work has been introduced officially (but is not applied everywhere)
- many formerly 'white' industrial jobs are now open to blacks
- black unions have been legalized
- blacks may now use public amenities like libraries, parks and swimming-pools.

But, in 1991, discrimination is still inherent in the political tricameral system of government: whites are guaranteed all political rights, the Coloureds and Indians some, whereas the blacks are granted virtually no political power except, to some degree, at local or regional levels.

Conservative whites say:

1. Changes must come slowly, as the country needs time to prepare the ground for equality: evolution is preferable to revolution.
2. Independent homelands in which blacks can live have been created.
3. Apartheid – which has virtually disappeared – means separateness: so what is wrong with separate states for separate races?
4. The 'underprivileged' sections of society must be convinced of the true merits of a free market economy.
5. Housing conditions have improved considerably.
6. South Africa is a 'bastion' of democracy – we whites, the superior race, 'God's chosen people', must on no account hand it over to any black extremist or guerrilla movement.

segregation	Trennung, Absonderung
criterion [kraɪ'tɪərɪən] *pl* **-ria**	Maßstab, Kriterium
category ['kætɪgərɪ]	Klasse
to abolish [ə'bɒlɪʃ]	abschaffen
interracial	zwischenrassisch
union	Gewerkschaft
amenity	Annehmlichkeit, *hier:* Einrichtung
discrimination	Benachteiligung, Diskriminierung
inherent [ɪn'hɪərənt]	innewohnend, eigen
tricameral [traɪ'kæmərəl]	Dreikammer-
virtually ['vɜ:tʃʊəlɪ]	praktisch
equality [i:'kwɒlətɪ]	Gleichheit
evolution	(allmähliche) Entwicklung
preferable ['prefərəbl] **to**	... vorzuziehen
homelands	Landgebiete für die Schwarzen (von der Regierung zugeteilt)
separateness ['seprətnɪs]	Getrenntsein
merits	*hier:* Vorzüge
housing conditions	Wohnverhältnisse
bastion ['bæstɪən]	Bastion
superior [su:'pɪərɪə]	überlegen
on no account	keinesfalls

Black protest:

1. Political reform is necessary: we demand the right to vote.
2. The 'independent' homelands, in which many of us live and which are hundreds of miles from the big cities, totally dependent on South Africa and for the most part infertile, are not a viable solution.
3. In the homelands we are deprived of our South African citizenship.
4. 'White' multinational capitalism dominates our lives and keeps wages for blacks low. We must do what the 'baas' wants us to do – it is 'whitey's world.
5. Our black children are deprived of a decent education, which means that they are kept ignorant.
6. Freedom from censorship, freedom of speech, freedom of assembly and the freedom of the press must be guaranteed to us forever.
7. Never again will we blacks tolerate repressive measures like arbitrary arrest, detention without trial, etc.
8. Many blacks boycott elections because elections have so far not provided any opportunity for real power-sharing at a national level.

Outlook:

There is the danger of an escalation of black unrest, which could result in the following chain of events:

demonstrations – boycotts of buses, schools, shops etc. – general strikes in the mining industries – terrorist incidents (bomb attacks, killings) – riots – upheaval/uprising – revolution – civil war.

However, the repeal of the apartheid acts and efforts to establish a non-racial, multi-party, democratic political system after the abolition of white minority rule are likely to pave the way for a constitution acceptable to all races in South Africa.

infertile [ɪn'fɜ:taɪl]	unfruchtbar
viable ['vaɪəbl]	machbar, realisierbar
to be deprived of something	um etwas gebracht werden
citizenship	Staatsangehörigkeit
whitey *(pej.)*	der, die Weiße
decent	anständig
ignorant ['ɪgnərənt]	unwissend, ungebildet
censorship	Zensur
freedom of assembly	Versammlungsfreiheit
arbitrary ['ɑ:bɪtrərɪ]	willkürlich
detention	Haft
trial	Prozeß (vor Gericht)
to boycott ['bɔɪkət]	boykottieren
election	Wahl
to provide	*hier:* bieten

escalation	Steigerung, Eskalation
incident	Zwischenfall
riot	Krawall
upheaval [ʌp'hi:vl]	Umsturz
uprising	Aufstand
civil war	Bürgerkrieg
repeal	Aufhebung (eines Gesetzes)
constitution	Verfassung

Education

Primary education in state schools:

While education for pre-school children in nursery schools is voluntary, compulsory schooling obliges British children of school age (between 5 and 16) to attend a primary school before proceeding to secondary school at eleven. The American equivalent for children between 6 and 12 is elementary school. In both countries formal education at this level stresses basic skills like the '3 Rs'.

A day at a British secondary school:

Pupils at a day school leave home in time to reach school by nine o'clock for morning assembly in the school hall, after which the first period begins. In the course of the morning and afternoon the teachers give

"En français, Jackson, en français."

nursery school	Kindergarten
compulsory schooling	Schulpflicht
to attend	besuchen
primary school *(BE)*	Grundschule
secondary school	höhere Schule
elementary school *(AE)*	Grundschule
the 'three Rs' (reading, writing and arithmetic)	die Grundfertigkeiten Lesen, Schreiben und Rechnen
day school	Tagesschule (Schule ohne Internat)
assembly	Versammlung der Schüler/innen und Lehrer/innen
school hall	Aula
period	Unterrichtsstunde

lessons in the various subjects on the curriculum, e.g. English language and literature, maths, a foreign language, social studies, music, art, science (physics, biology and chemistry), history, geography, PE (physical education) etc. The school day ends between 3 and 4 pm, when all pupils except boarders in public schools can go home.

Many pupils are involved in extra-curricular activities like acting or singing in the school choir.

A year at a British secondary school:

After the summer holidays the first term begins and work starts on the year's syllabus. The topics, texts and subjects to be studied vary according to which stream pupils at comprehensive schools have been placed in. Tests are given regularly so that continuous assessment can be made of a pupil's performance. Written and oral examinations must be taken/sat. A wide range of non-academic subjects is also offered: CDT (craft, design, technology), information technology, metalwork, home economics, carpentry etc. At the end of the third term, just before school breaks up for the summer holidays, pupils receive their school reports with their marks.

School-leaving examinations in Britain:

Pupils not interested in an academic career may decide to leave school at about 16, after completing the fifth form. They have a better chance of finding employment in commerce and industry, for which they have been prepared by vocational guidance and vocational training, if they have passed the General Certificate of Secondary Education (GCSE). This examination has replaced both the Certificate of Secondary Education (CSE) and the General Certificate of Education (GCE) O (Ordinary) level.

Academically-minded pupils may, after passing this lower-level exam, choose to spend two years in the sixth form and specialize in the subjects for which they show an aptitude. Those who make the grade by passing two (or more) A (Advanced) levels have qualified for entrance to university or other higher education.

subject	Fach
curriculum [kə'rɪkjʊləm]	Lehrplan (Fächerangebot einer Schule)
social studies	Gesellschaftskunde
boarder	Internatsschüler/in
public school	höhere Privatschule
extra-curricular	außerhalb des Stundenplans, außerplanmäßig
to act	(eine Rolle) spielen
choir ['kwaɪə]	Chor
term	*hier:* Trimester
syllabus ['sɪləbəs]	Lehrplan (Liste d. Fächer, Themen, Bücher, Texte etc. eines Schuljahres)
stream	Leistungsgruppe
comprehensive school	Gesamtschule
assessment	Leistungsmessung
performance	Leistung
oral	mündlich
to sit an examination	eine Prüfung machen
craft	Werkunterricht
information technology	Informationstechnik
metalwork	Metallverarbeitung
home economics	Hauswirtschaft
carpentry ['kɑːpəntrɪ]	Werken (mit Holz)
to break up	*hier:* aufhören, schließen
school report	Schulzeugnis
mark *(BE)*	Note
career [kə'rɪə]	Laufbahn, Beruf
form	Klasse
vocational guidance	Berufsberatung
vocational training	Berufsausbildung
aptitude	Begabung, Talent
to make the grade	'es schaffen'
to pass (an examination)	(eine Prüfung) bestehen

Tertiary education:

After passing their entrance examination, those people wishing to continue their education at university or college level enrol at a university, polytechnic or other institution of higher (= tertiary) education which awards diplomas or degrees in a wide variety of fields such as medicine, law, economics, computer science etc. Some universities in Britain and the USA enjoy particular prestige, e.g. Oxbridge (Oxford and Cambridge) or the American 'Ivy League' universities like Harvard, Princeton and Yale, all of which can afford to select only those students with the best grades.

Many students live on the campus, especially first-year and second-year students (US: freshmen and sophomores), while third-year and fourth-year students (US: juniors and seniors) usually rent rooms or flats elsewhere. After three years of study undergraduates who have successfully participated in seminars and tutorials and attended lectures sit their examinations. Those who pass are awarded a bachelor's degree in Arts (B.A.), Science (B.Sc.) etc, depending on what subjects they have majored in. After graduating they may choose to devote an additional year to studying for a master's degree (M.A., M.Sc. etc.), which often includes writing a thesis. They may then do postgraduate research and write a dissertation for a doctorate or a doctor's degree (Ph.D. etc.).

Topical issues in education:

- the threat of a possible decline in educational standards,
- a growth in violence at inner-city schools, especially in the USA,
- the problem of drug abuse and drug addiction in US schools,
- the tendency of more and more pupils to drop out of school,
- an increase in truancy,
- a teacher shortage in some subjects, a surplus in other subjects,
- a chronic shortage of money invested by the state in its schools, in laboratories, books, equipment etc.

tertiary ['tɜːʃərɪ]	tertiär, Hochschul-
to enrol	sich einschreiben, immatrikulieren
to award [ə'wɔːd]	zuerkennen, verleihen
degree	akademischer Grad
economics	Volkswirtschaft
computer science	Informatik
prestige [pre'stiːʒ]	Ansehen, Prestige
grade *(AE)*	Note
campus	Gesamtanlage einer Universität oder eines College
undergraduate	Student/in (ohne Abschlußexamen)
tutorial [tjuː'tɔːrɪəl]	Tutorenkurs
lecture	Vorlesung
to major in	als Hauptfach studieren
to graduate	einen akademischen Grad erhalten
thesis ['θiːsɪs]	wissenschaftliche Arbeit
postgraduate [ˌpəʊst'grædʒʊət] **research**	Weiterstudieren nach Erlangen eines akademischen Grades
dissertation	wissenschaftliche Abhandlung, Dissertation
doctorate	Doktortitel, Doktorwürde
doctor's degree	Doktorwürde
drug abuse [ə'bjuːs]	Drogenmißbrauch
to drop out	(die Schule) abbrechen
truancy	(Schul-)Schwänzerei
shortage	Mangel
surplus ['sɜːpləs]	Überschuß
to invest	investieren
laboratory [BE: lə'bɒrətərɪ]	Labor

Religion

Basic information:

There are hundreds of millions of Christians in the world, most of them in Europe and North and South America. Catholicism and Protestantism have won many adherents in the Third World, where large numbers of heathens, i.e. those who do not believe in one of the chief religions like Judaism, Hinduism, Islam or Christianity, have been converted to Christianity by missionaries. Today, however, the number of people actually practising their Christian faith is on the decline, so that the mainline churches are losing more and more members of their congregations.

In Britain and the US, where nobody may be discriminated against on religious grounds, complete freedom of religious persuasion and expression is regarded as a basic human right to be enjoyed by every citizen. Similarly, as there is no obligation to believe in God, unbelievers such as atheists and agnostics are in no way excluded from full participation in national life. Religious tolerance in Britain is also extended to the millions of coloured immigrants, including Muslims/Moslems from Pakistan, Hindus from India and Rastafarians from Jamaica etc.

Christian ['krɪstʃən]	Christ/in
Catholicism [kə'θɒlɪsɪzəm]	Katholizismus
Protestantism	Protestantismus
adherent [əd'hɪərənt]	Anhänger/in
heathen ['hiːðən]	Heide
Judaism ['dʒuːdeɪɪzəm]	jüdische Religion
Christianity	Christentum
to convert	bekehren
missionary	Missionar/in
faith	Glaube
mainline	Haupt-
congregation	Kirchengemeinde, -mitglieder
to discriminate against	benachteiligen
persuasion	Überzeugung
unbeliever	Ungläubige(r)
atheist ['eɪθɪɪst]	Atheist/in
agnostic	Agnostiker/in
Rastafarian [ˌræstə'feərɪən]	Angehörige(r) einer Glaubensgemeinschaft, die sich auf den früheren äthiopischen Kaiser Haile Selassie beruft

Anglicanism is the established religion in England, so that the Church of England, the Anglican Church, is the established Church. It separated from the Roman (Catholic) Church in the 16th century, when King Henry VIII repudiated the supremacy of the Pope and dissolved the monasteries. Although the monarch is the head of the Anglican Church and although monarchs are traditionally crowned by the Archbishop of Canterbury in Westminster Abbey, Anglicanism does not play a role comparable to that of Islam in the Arab countries; it is not an official state religion.

While the main denomination in Scotland and Northern Ireland is Presbyterianism, many citizens of the UK, e.g. Methodists and Baptists, are members of other Protestant Nonconformist denominations. The only real exception to peaceful religious co-existence is the sectarian strife between Catholics and Protestants in Northern Ireland. Elsewhere in the UK the positive effects of the ecumenical movement are plainly visible.

In the US, where religion has a greater influence on social life, there is even more religious pluralism than in Britain. While Roman Catholics constitute the largest single denomination in the US, there is also a wide variety of free and independent Protestant Churches: Baptists, Methodists, Lutherans, Quakers, Episcopalians, Presbyterians, Congregationalists, Mormons, Adventists etc. Groups like the Evangelicals place particular emphasis on Scripture (especially the Gospel) and faith in Christ rather than on ritual and ceremony. Revival meetings organized by evangelists in search of converts and often broadcast on TV are also a common feature of religious life in the US.

Freedom of religion has attracted innumerable immigrants to North America since the 17th century, many of them victims of religious persecution in their native countries in Europe. Thus, for example, the millions of Jews living in the US have found a haven in which they can practise their Jewish faith in temples and synagogues under the spiritual guidance of their rabbis without having to fear the excesses of radical anti-Semitism.

Religious life in a Christian family

Shortly after birth a child is christened or baptized in the presence of its godfather or godmother and is thus received into the Christian Church. Religious upbringing and religious instruction or education (R.E. as a subject at school) are the responsibility of the Church, the parents and

Anglican Church	anglikanische Kirche
to separate	(sich) trennen
Roman (Catholic) Church	römisch-katholische Kirche
supremacy [su:'preməsɪ]	Oberhoheit
the Pope	der Papst
to dissolve [dɪ'zɒlv]	auflösen
monastery ['mɒnəstrɪ]	(Männer-)Kloster
monarch ['mɒnək]	Monarch/in
archbishop ['ɑ:tʃ'bɪʃəp]	Erzbischof
Canterbury	Zentrum der anglikanischen Kirche
comparable ['kɒmpərəbl]	vergleichbar
denomination	Bekenntnis, Konfession
Presbyterianism	Glaubensgemeinschaft der Presbyterianer
Methodist	Methodist/in
Baptist	Baptist/in
Nonconformist	nichtanglikanisch
sectarian	konfessionell
strife	Zwist, Hader, Streit
ecumenical [ˌi:kjʊ'menɪkl]	ökumenisch
pluralism	Vielfalt, Pluralismus
Evangelical [ˌɪvæn'dʒelɪkl]	Anhänger/in einer konservativen und fundamentalistischen Bewegung, Evangelikaler/in
Scripture ['skrɪptʃə]	die Heilige Schrift
Gospel	Evangelium
ritual ['rɪtjʊəl]	Ritual
revival meeting	Erweckungsversammlung
evangelist [ɪ'vændʒəlɪst]	Massenbekehrungsprediger/in
convert	Bekehrte(r)
persecution	Verfolgung
Jew	Jude/Jüdin
synagogue ['sɪnəgɒg]	Synagoge
rabbi ['ræbaɪ]	Rabbiner

to christen ['krɪsn]	taufen
to baptize [bæp'taɪz]	taufen
godfather/godmother	Taufpate/Taufpatin
upbringing	Erziehung

the school. A baptized child should be taught how to lead a good Christian life, become acquainted with the Old and New Testaments of the Bible and learn the Lord's Prayer and the Creed. At about the age of 13, a Protestant child can be confirmed, thereby becoming a full member of the Church and thus entitled to receive Holy Communion.

Pious churchgoers attend church services on Sundays to worship God. They listen to the sermon given by the clergyman preaching from the pulpit, pray to the Maker/Creator, sing hymns and donate money to the charity organizations run by the Church. Devout Catholics also go to confession regularly to tell the priest their sins in the confessional. A Christian's spiritual leader may be a Catholic priest, an Anglican vicar or rector, or, in the case of Presbyterian and some other Nonconformist Churches, a minister or pastor.

Contemporary trends in Christian Churches

1. A general decline in church attendance and membership has become evident.
2. There is now a widening gap between extremely liberal tendencies among clerics and church members at one end of the scale and very conservative tendencies at the other end.
3. There has been a spread of fundamentalism in the US and a consequent growth in the popularity of the US televangelists. These preachers manipulate television in order to express their puritanical views and to attack various aspects of the permissive society such as greater sexual freedom, women's liberation etc. Their fundamentalist belief in the literal truth of the Bible has even led them to oppose the teaching of Darwin's theory of evolution.
4. The fear of failing to attract the young is one of the main concerns of Churches today.
5. More and more people have come to regard religion as a private and personal matter concerning only the individual and God, which explains the growing reluctance to worship in churches.

the Lord's Prayer [preə]	das Vaterunser
the Creed	das Glaubensbekenntnis, Credo
to confirm	konfirmieren
Holy Communion	Abendmahl, Eucharistie
pious	fromm
to attend	besuchen
service	Gottesdienst
to worship ['wɜ:ʃɪp]	anbeten, verehren
sermon	Predigt
clergyman ['klɜ:dʒɪmən]	Geistliche(r)
to preach	predigen
pulpit ['pʊlpit]	Kanzel
to pray	beten
the Maker/Creator	der Schöpfer
hymn [hɪm]	Kirchenlied, Choral
to donate	spenden, opfern
charity	wohltätig, karitativ
devout [dɪ'vaʊt]	fromm, gläubig
to go to confession	zur Beichte gehen
priest [prɪ:st]	Priester
sin	Sünde
confessional	Beichtstuhl
vicar ['vɪkə]**/rector**	anglikanischer Pfarrer
minister/pastor	Pfarrer/in

attendance	Besuch, *hier:* Besucherzahl
gap	Abstand
cleric	Geistliche(r), Kleriker/in
fundamentalism	christliche Bewegung, die sich streng auf den Wortlaut der Bibel beruft

televangelist [telɪ'vændʒəlɪst]	Fernsehprediger/in
preacher	Prediger/in
to manipulate [mə'nɪpjʊleɪt]	geschickt handhaben, manipulieren
puritanical	übertrieben sittenstreng, puritanisch
permissive	*hier:* tolerant, liberal
literal	wortwörtlich, buchstäblich
concern	Anliegen, Sorge

The danger of sects

Fundamentalist sects are by no means a new phenomenon, but in the last few decades some radical sects – often characterized by occult and sinister practices and rituals – have emerged, especially in the US. Dissatisfied with the mainstream religions, which frequently seem unable to provide answers to their moral and ethical questions, many young people are attracted to such radical sects. With the help of mind-control techniques similar to brainwashing, the leaders of the sects have little difficulty in exploiting the feelings and emotional needs of young people, in destroying their self-respect and individuality and in making them mentally and emotionally dependent.

sect	Sekte
phenomenon [fɪˈnɒmɪnən]	Erscheinung, Phänomen
occult [ɒˈkʌlt]	geheim, magisch, okkult
sinister	finster, unheimlich
to emerge [ɪˈmɜːdʒ]	entstehen
mainstream	Haupt-, etabliert
mind control	Manipulation des Denkens
technique [tekˈniːk]	Methode, Verfahren, Technik
brainwashing	Gehirnwäsche
to exploit	ausnutzen, ausbeuten
self-respect	Selbstachtung

The crime rate is rising

Crime and its causes

Another death penalty debate in Parliament

Crime and Punishment

Some crimes:	(committed by)	criminals:
theft		thief
burglary		burglar
armed bank-robbery		bank-robber
mugging		mugger
drug trafficking		drug trafficker
espionage		spy
hijacking (e.g. a plane)		hijacker
taking s.o. hostage/kidnapping		kidnapper
rape		rapist
murder/homicide		murderer

In addition to such criminal offences, there are also civil cases which do not involve public prosecution but are dealt with by civil courts.

The judicial process: justice and the criminal

If successful, police arrest the criminals/offenders/ perpetrators/ culprits. Their cases are taken to court:

1. The detained suspect comes up before the examining magistrate(s).
2. A suit is filed if there are adequate grounds for suspicion.

crime rate	Verbrechensrate
death penalty ['penltɪ]	Todesstrafe

to commit a crime	ein Verbrechen begehen
criminal	Verbrecher/in
theft	Diebstahl
burglary	Einbruch
armed bank-robbery	bewaffneter Bankraub
mugging	Raubüberfall (auf der Straße)
drug trafficking	Drogenhandel
espionage [ˌespɪə'nɑːʒ]	Spionage
to hijack	entführen
to take s.o. hostage ['hɒstɪdʒ]	jmdn. als Geisel nehmen
rape	Vergewaltigung
murder	Mord
homicide ['hɒmɪsaɪd]	Mord, Totschlag
offence	Vergehen
civil case	Zivilsache
public prosecution	Anklagevertretung durch Staatsanwalt
civil court	Zivilgericht
the judicial [dʒuː'dɪʃl] **process**	das Wirken der Justiz
justice	Gerechtigkeit, Recht
offender	Missetäter, Straffälliger
perpetrator	Täter/in
culprit ['kʌlprɪt]	Täter/in
to take a case to court	eine Sache vor Gericht bringen
to detain [-'-]	in (Untersuchungs-)Haft behalten, festnehmen
suspect ['sʌspekt]	Verdächtige(r)
examining magistrate ['mædʒɪstreɪt]	Untersuchungsrichter(in)
to file a suit [suːt]	Klage einreichen
adequate ['ædɪkwət]	angemessen, hinreichend

3. The suspect is accused of / charged with a crime at a lawcourt.
4. The defendant stands trial/ goes on trial for the crime she or he is accused of.

The prosecution:

The public prosecutor / district attorney tries to prove the defendant's guilt beyond all reasonable doubt so that he/she will be convicted. Witnesses testify (sometimes on oath) in the witness-box/-stand.

The accused/defendant:

The accused is in the dock. If he/she pleads 'not guilty' and does not confess the crime, the defence barrister / counsel for the defence calls witnesses in order to exonerate the accused. The counsel for the defence and the prosecution may cross-examine each other's witnesses. The defence counsel or the accused, if he or she has pleaded guilty, may appeal to the judge for clemency on the grounds of extenuating circumstances.

Trial by jury:

The judge may examine both sides and question the validity or relevance of any evidence or circumstantial evidence. After the closing speeches of both sides the jury (normally 12 jurors, who have sat in the jury-box during the trial) have to consider the verdict.

If the jury returns a verdict of not guilty, the accused is cleared of a crime, acquitted and freed.

If the jury returns a verdict of guilty, the accused may be fined, placed on probation or (if it is a case of juvenile delinquency) be sent to Borstal/a reformatory. Other criminals are sentenced to some months'/years' imprisonment or even to life imprisonment. In some countries the death penalty (capital punishment) is in force. In such countries criminals are sentenced to death for capital offences.

to accuse s.o. of a crime	jmdn. eines Verbrechens anklagen
to charge s.o. with a crime	jmdn. eines Verbrechens beschuldigen
lawcourt	Gericht(shof)
defendant	Angeklagte(r)
to stand trial	vor Gericht stehen
public prosecutor *(BE)*	Staatsanwalt/Staatsanwältin
district attorney [ə'tɜ:nɪ] *(AE)*	Staatsanwalt/Staatsanwältin
guilt	Schuld
to convict	überführen
witness	Zeuge/Zeugin
to testify	bezeugen, aussagen
on oath	unter Eid
witness-box/-stand	Zeugenstand
in the dock	auf der Anklagebank
to plead guilty	sich schuldig bekennen
to confess	gestehen
defence barrister	Verteidiger/in
counsel for the defence	Verteidiger/in
to exonerate [ɪg'zɒnəreɪt]	entlasten
to cross-examine	ins Kreuzverhör nehmen
clemency	Milde
extenuating circumstances ['sɜ:kəmstənsəs]	mildernde Umstände
trial by jury ['dʒʊərɪ]	Schwurgerichtsverhandlung
judge [dʒʌdʒ]	Richter/in
validity [ˌvə'lɪdətɪ]	Richtigkeit, Stichhaltigkeit
evidence	Beweis(mittel), Beweise
circumstantial [ˌsɜ:kəm'stænʃl] **evidence**	Indizienbeweis(e)
jury	Jury
juror ['dʒʊərə]	Geschworene(r), Mitglied der Jury
verdict ['vɜ:dɪkt]	Urteil (der Geschworenen)
to clear of	freisprechen von
to acquit	freisprechen, für unschuldig erklären
to fine	mit einer Geldstrafe belegen
to place on probation	auf Bewährung entlassen
juvenile delinquency [dɪ'lɪŋkwənsɪ]	Jugendkriminalität
Borstal *(GB)*	Jugendstrafanstalt
reformatory [rɪ'fɔ:mətərɪ]	Besserungsanstalt
to sentence to	verurteilen zu
imprisonment	Gefängnis, Haft
capital punishment	Todesstrafe

Methods of execution:

A criminal who has been given the death penalty may be
- electrocuted in the electric chair
- lethally injected
- beheaded
- hanged by a hangman or shot by a firing-squad.

In prison a convict may spend his or her time
- waiting to be reprieved or pardoned
- hoping that his or her case will be reconsidered if he or she has appealed to a higher court and is awaiting a new trial
- waiting for execution on death row if he or she is under sentence of death.

Capital punishment/the death penalty:

Capital punishment has been abolished in most countries (it was abandoned in England in 1965). As a result of the rising crime rates, the 'pro-hanging' lobby is growing stronger. Some people would like to have capital punishment restored/reintroduced: they demand retaliation, retribution and vengeance.

Arguments put forward in favour of capital punishment:

1. It is an expression of society's moral outrage at particularly offensive crimes; in this way a criminal meets with his or her 'just deserts'.
2. It may serve as a deterrent to others.
3. It reduces the costs of keeping prisoners sentenced to life imprisonment in the already overcrowded prison cells.

Arguments put forward against capital punishment:

1. Crime rates have proved to be unaffected in countries in which capital punishment is in force, so it does not work as a deterrent.
2. A system of justice based on the principle of 'an eye for an eye' is inhumane and an offence against human dignity.
3. There is no absolute certainty that the convicted murderer actually committed the crime because no legal system is foolproof.
4. It may create martyrs who can be exploited by radical movements (for example by the IRA in Northern Ireland).

execution [ˌeksɪˈkjuːʃn]	Hinrichtung
to electrocute	auf dem elektrischen Stuhl hinrichten
to be lethally injected	eine tödliche Spritze bekommen
to behead [bɪˈhed]	enthaupten, köpfen
firing-squad	Exekutionskommando
to reprieve	begnadigen
to pardon	begnadigen
to reconsider	*hier:* wiederaufnehmen
to appeal	Berufung einlegen
on death row [rəʊ]	in der Todeszelle
to abolish [əˈbɒlɪʃ]	abschaffen
to abandon [əˈbændən]	aufgeben
to restore	wiederherstellen
to reintroduce	wiedereinführen
retaliation [rɪˌtælɪˈeɪʃən]	Vergeltung, Vergeltungsschlag
retribution	Vergeltung, ausgleichende Gerechtigkeit
vengeance [ˈvendʒəns]	Rache
moral outrage [ˈaʊtreɪdʒ]	moralische Entrüstung
offensive	abstoßend
just deserts [dɪˈzɜːts]	wohlverdiente Strafe
deterrent	Abschreckung
prison cell	Gefängniszelle
unaffected	unberührt, unbeeinflußt
inhumane [ˌɪnhjuːˈmeɪn]	unmenschlich
human dignity	Menschenwürde
foolproof	narrensicher, *hier:* absolut sicher
martyr [ˈmɑːtə]	Märtyrer
to exploit	ausnutzen, Kapital schlagen aus

Crime prevention as a general problem:

To discourage potential criminals some countries want to
- humanize the judicial system,
- set up more rehabilitation programmes and provide more psychiatric counselling,
- be more lenient with criminals, especially first offenders

Others take a hard line against 'soft' laws. They want
- to prevent the liberalization of penal laws and are opposed to penal reforms,
- tougher law enforcement,
- capital punishment to be restored.

to discourage	abschrecken, abhalten
to humanize	menschlicher, humaner machen
judicial [dʒuːˈdɪʃəl] **system**	Rechtssystem
rehabilitation	Rehabilitation, soziale Wiedereingliederung
psychiatric [ˌsaɪkɪˈætrɪk] **counselling**	psychiatrische Beratung
lenient [ˈliːnjənt]	mild(e), nachsichtig
first offender	nicht Vorbestrafte(r)
liberalization	Liberalisierung
penal [ˈpiːnl] **law**	Strafrecht
tough [tʌf]	hart, streng
law enforcement	Vollstreckung, Durchsetzung von Gesetzen

Spectators run amok

Violence on the terraces

Bloody Saturdays

Hooligans strike again

War against hooligans

Football Hooliganism

Basic information:

Violence has often been connected with certain sporting events. But crowd violence or hooliganism in and around the football stadiums has escalated in recent years. Off and on the pitches there have been mass arrests of fanatical football supporters at matches. In 1985 English football hooligans provoked riots which led to the deaths of 39 people at the Heysel Stadium in Brussels, Belgium. English football clubs – not the

spectator	Zuschauer/in
to run amok [ə'mɒk]	Amok laufen
terraces	Stehplätze
hooligan	Rowdy
to strike	*hier:* zuschlagen

hooliganism	Rowdytum
event	Ereignis
stadium	Stadion
to escalate ['eskəleɪt]	sich steigern
pitch	Spielfeld
mass arrests	Massenverhaftungen
fanatical	fanatisch
to provoke	provozieren
riot	Krawall

Scottish, Welsh or Irish clubs – were excluded from European competitions and tournaments for some years. The European football associations are now looking for the reasons for and solutions to the problem of football hooliganism in their respective countries.

On account of football hooligans/thugs/yobs England's image has suffered serious damage worldwide.

The parties involved in a typical confrontation:

On one side:

supporters/fans of the home team

On the other side:

rival supporters/fans of the opposing team/the visiting team

Police forces intervene

There are often mounted police in riot gear with truncheons and dogs. They form security cordons to separate the two groups of fans.

A possible sequence of events:

The hooligans
- set off fireworks and start brawling on the terraces,
- rip out seats and use them as weapons,
- assault rival fans and attack police.

The hooligans run amok, cause mayhem or go on the rampage: on their way home the looting and marauding gangs smash windows, cause all kinds of damage and even vandalize the train on the return journey.

The police try to arrest the worst offenders. There are sometimes many casualties; a lot of people are injured and some may even die.

The cirumstances in which such situations arise:
- during the soccer season
- at home matches and away matches
- at club friendlies abroad
- at Cup matches: Champions' Cup, Cupwinners' Cup and UEFA Cup
- at European or World championships.

to exclude	ausschließen
competition	Wettbewerb
tournament ['tʊənəmənt]	Turnier
association [əˌsəʊsɪ'eɪʃn]	Vereinigung
respective	jeweilig
thug	Schlägertyp
yob [jɒb]	Lümmel

home team	Heimmannschaft
opposing team	gegnerisches Team
police forces	Polizeikräfte
to intervene	eingreifen
mounted	beritten
riot gear	Kampfausrüstung
truncheon ['trʌntʃən]	Schlagstock
security cordon ['kɔ:dn]	Absperrkette
to set off fireworks	Feuerwerkskörper anzünden
brawling	Schlägereien
to rip out	herausreißen
to assault	angreifen
to cause mayhem ['meɪhem]	Chaos verursachen
to go on the rampage [ræm'peɪdʒ]	sich austoben, herumwüten
to loot	plündern
to maraud [mə'rɔ:d]	plündern, marodieren
to smash	einschlagen
to vandalize	(mutwillig) zerstören
offender	Übeltäter/in
casualty ['kæʒjʊəltɪ]	Opfer (sowohl Verletzte als auch Tote)
cirumstances ['sɜ:kəmstənsɪz]	Umstände
soccer	Fußball
away match	Auswärtsspiel
friendly	Freundschaftsspiel
cup	Pokal
champion	Meister/in
cupwinner	Pokalsieger/in
UEFA	Europäische Fußballvereinigung
championships	Meisterschaften, Meisterschaftskämpfe

A comprehensive package of measures to ensure that reasonable precautions are taken requires that the authorities

1. separate rival supporters in the stadium,
2. impose tougher crowd control; everyone at the grounds must be searched for potential weapons,
3. change the existing football stadiums into all-seater stadiums,
4. restrict the sale of alcohol within the stadium and in the vicinity of the grounds,
5. bar known troublemakers from entering the stadium,
6. introduce the distribution of compulsory membership/ID cards,
7. install closed-circuit TV (CCTV) in order to have fan groups under constant video surveillance and to make it easier to identify troublemakers,
8. impose harsher penalties or even maximum sentences on hooligans, including prison and detention centre terms,
9. 'fine' a club a number of penalty points or relegate it to a lower division.

Possible reasons for hooliganism:

1. Unemployment: many unemployed young people with deprived backgrounds rid themselves of their emotional and physical frustration; they give vent to their aggression in the stadium.
2. Sometimes there are not enough policemen in attendance at the football grounds.
3. Right-wing National Front supporters eager to provoke riots are present in the stadiums.
4. A wrong interpretation of what it means to be a patriot (for example 'I'm proud of being England's worst thug').

comprehensive package	Gesamtpaket
to ensure	sicherstellen
precautions	Vorsichtsmaßnahmen
to impose	*hier:* zwangsweise einführen
tough [tʌf]	streng
all-seater stadium	Stadion nur mit Sitzplätzen
vicinity	Nachbarschaft, Nähe
to bar	ausschließen
compulsory	zwangsmäßig, obligatorisch
membership card	Mitgliedskarte
ID (identity) card	Ausweis(karte)
closed-circuit TV ['sɜ:kɪt]	Fernsehüberwachungsanlage
video surveillance [sɜ:'veɪləns]	Videoüberwachung
harsher penalty	härtere Strafe
maximum sentence	Höchststrafe
detention centre	Jugendstrafanstalt
term	*hier:* Freiheitsstrafe
to fine	*hier:* mit Punktabzug bestrafen
to relegate	*hier:* absteigen lassen
division	Liga

with deprived backgrounds	aus ärmlichen Verhältnissen, sozial benachteiligt
to rid oneself of	sich freimachen von
to give vent to	(seiner Aggression) Luft machen
in attendance	im Dienst, in Bereitschaft
National Front [frʌnt]	rechtsradikale Organisation (u. a. auch 'Skinheads')
patriot ['pætrɪət]	Patriot/in

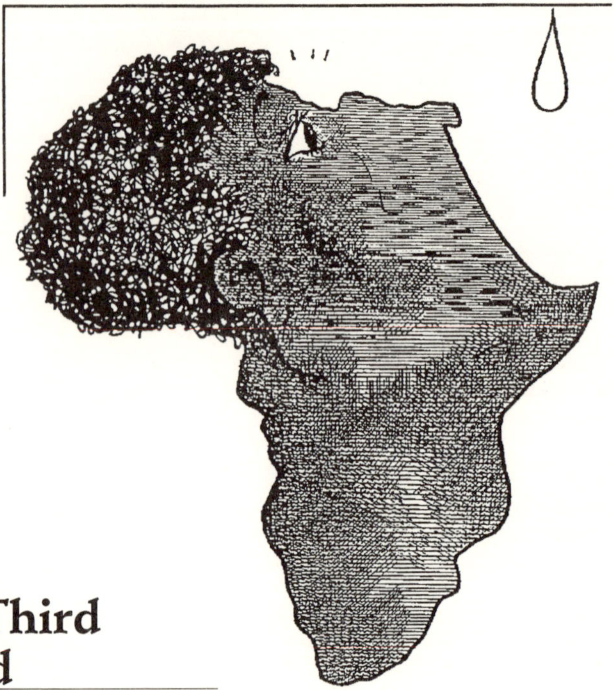

The Third World

Basic information:

Nearly all countries in tropical and subtropical regions are developing countries (except such countries as Australia, New Zealand and South Africa). Some are borderline cases e.g. Taiwan, South Korea, Indonesia, Brazil, Chile or Argentina.

Most countries in the North are 'developed' (i.e. have risen to a higher economic level), e.g. Europe, North America and Japan. There is a 'North-South divide' separating about 20 industrialized countries from more than 100 major or minor developing countries at various stages of economic advance.

Hardest hit are the African continent and South-East Asia; South America is slightly better off (no overpopulation as in India, for example). Some of the 'worst cases' are Mali, Chad, Niger, Burkina Faso, Sudan, Ethiopia, Bangladesh, Burma and Haiti.

tropical	tropisch
subtropical	subtropisch
developing country	Entwicklungsland
borderline case	Grenzfall, *hier:* Schwellenland
Indonesia [ˌɪndəʊˈniːzjə]	Indonesien
divide	Spalt, Kluft
industrialized	industrialisiert
stage	Stadium, Stufe
overpopulation	Überbevölkerung
Ethiopia [ˌiːθɪˈəʊpjə]	Äthiopien

Physical features of Third-World countries:

Climate – their tropical or subtropical climate means that these countries are either too hot and humid or so dry that they suffer from scarcity of water and periodic droughts.

Vegetation – rainforests, savanna(h), steppes and deserts.

Natural catastrophes – floods in delta regions, droughts around the rim of the Sahara, volcanic eruptions and earthquakes in and around mountainous regions.

Typical political structures of many developing countries:

1. autocratic/authoritarian rulers or ruling élites,
2. tribalism, nepotism and corruption,
3. one-party systems rather than real multi-party systems,
4. over-centralization and excessive bureaucracy,
5. military coups d'état (sometimes civil war in regions held by rebels),
6. disrespect for human rights.

Common social problems of developing countries:

1. excessive population growth: an average of 2–4 per cent a year,
2. starvation and malnutrition: lack of vitamins, low intake of calories and protein,
3. a high rate of illiteracy,
4. low life expectancy: between 40 and 50 years on an average,
5. high infant mortality rates,
6. widespread diseases and epidemics: cholera, malaria, Aids, typhoid, dysentery, measles, whooping cough etc.,
7. lack of water and sanitation: poor hygienic conditions, often contaminated water,

feature	Merkmal
climate ['klaımıt]	Klima
humid ['hju:mıd]	feucht
scarcity ['skeəsətı]	Mangel
drought [draʊt]	Dürre
vegetation [vədʒı'teıʃn]	Pflanzenwelt, Vegetation
rainforest	Regenwald
steppe [step]	Steppe
desert ['dezət]	Wüste
catastrophe [kə'tæstrəfı]	Katastrophe
flood [flʌd]	Überflutung, Überschwemmung
rim	Rand
volcanic [vɒl'kænık] **eruption**	Vulkanausbruch
earthquake	Erdbeben

autocratic	despotisch, autokratisch
élite [eı'li:t]	Führungsschicht, Elite
tribalism	etwa: Stammesrivalitäten
nepotism	Vetternwirtschaft, Nepotismus
over-centralization	*hier:* zu starre Planwirtschaft
bureaucracy [bjʊə'rɒkrəsı]	Bürokratie
coup d'état [ˌku:deı'tɑ:]	Staatsstreich
civil war	Bürgerkrieg
rebel [rebl]	Aufständischer, Rebell
human rights	Menschenrechte

starvation	Hunger, Hungertod
malnutrition [ˌmælnju:'trıʃn]	Unterernährung
protein	Eiweiß
illiteracy [ı'lıtərəsı]	Analphabetentum
life expectancy	Lebenserwartung
infant mortality	Säuglingssterblichkeit
epidemic	Epidemie
typhoid ['taıfɔıd]	Typhus
dysentery ['dısntrı]	Ruhr
measles	Masern
whooping cough ['hu:pıŋ kɒf]	Keuchhusten
sanitation	sanitäre Einrichtungen
hygienic [haı'dʒi:nık]	hygienisch
contaminated	verseucht, verunreinigt

8. poor housing conditions: millions of people are homeless or live in slums (shanties/shacks made of cardboard and corrugated iron etc); they are slum-dwellers,
9. migrations from rural to urban areas: peasants leave their land or disaster-hit regions and migrate to famine shelters/refugee camps or to the big cities, where they end up in slums,
10. general attitude towards work: widespread fatalism, a hand-to-mouth existence, little interest in long-term projects without immediate profit.

Economic problems:

1. Lack or absence of raw materials or natural resources like gold, iron ore, crude oil, copper, tin, bauxite, uranium,
2. inadequate infrastructure (railways, ports, roads, hospitals, schools etc),
3. lack of technical equipment, machinery and native-born experts/specialists: engineers, technicians, spare parts must be 'imported',
4. huge foreign debts which they are unable to repay and which drain export earnings,
5. a large rural sector, a small industrial sector and an expanding service sector,
6. low commodity prices for their export products, high prices for necessary import products.

Agricultural problems:

1. The destruction of ecosystems: for example, burning tropical forests to gain farmland results in soil exhaustion; there is a lack of ecologically beneficial agriculture,
2. soil erosion, lack of soil fertility: loss of topsoil – desertification – infertile land,

housing conditions	Wohnverhältnisse
slum	Elendsviertel, Slum
shanty/shack	Hütte, Baracke
cardboard	Pappe
corrugated iron	Wellblech
slum-dweller	Slumbewohner
migration	Wanderung
rural	ländlich
urban	städtisch
peasant ['peznt]	(Klein)Bauer
disaster-hit	Katastrophen-
famine shelter/refugee camp	Flüchtlingslager
fatalism ['feɪtəlɪzəm]	Fatalismus

raw material	Rohstoff
natural resources	Bodenschätze
iron ore ['aɪən ɔ:]	Eisenerz
crude oil	Rohöl
copper	Kupfer
tin	Zinn
bauxite ['bɔ:ksaɪt]	Bauxit
uranium	Uran
inadequate [ɪn'ædɪkwət]	unzureichend
infrastructure	Infrastruktur
spare parts	Ersatzteile
foreign debts	Auslandsschulden
to drain	entleeren, *hier:* aufzehren
service sector	Dienstleistungssektor
commodity [kə'mɒdɪtɪ]	Ware

ecosystem	Ökosystem
soil exhaustion	Bodenerschöpfung
ecologically beneficial	*hier:* umweltschonend
soil erosion	Bodenabtragung
soil fertility	Bodenfruchtbarkeit
topsoil	Humusschicht, -boden
desertification [dɪˌzɜ:tɪfɪ'keɪʃən]	Versteppung, Wüstwerdung
infertile [ɪn'fɜ:taɪl]	unfruchtbar

3. monocultural farming of cash crops for export like coffee, tea, cocoa, tobacco, soybeans etc.,
4. the destruction of self-sufficient economies: there are not enough traditional crops like sorghum or millet,
5. an insufficiency or misuse of fertilizers, pesticides, insecticides and disinfectants to fight locust infestations and other pests,
6. a small number of rich landowners own most of the land while millions of poor peasants have to share the rest (often infertile land),
7. a high rate of unemployed or under-employed people, which results in migrations to the big cities.

Third-World countries argue:

The natural resources in our countries are exploited. The industrialized countries pay unfair prices for our raw materials. They buy them very cheap, refine them in their home countries, process them into finished products and sell them on the world markets (and to our developing countries) at high prices.

The rich countries dominate the world markets and dictate the prices for the products which come from our poor countries. They act as if we were still colonies. They even set up import barriers on products from our countries and in this way make our products more expensive. There is excessive production, waste and affluence in the First World, hunger, poverty, misery and starvation in the Third World.

How aid to developing countries could be put to good use:

1. Try to limit population growth by encouraging family planning,
2. spend a higher percentage of the GNP (gross national product) of a country on foreign aid (the optimum amount would be one per cent or more),
3. give preference not to large-scale infrastructure projects but to small-scale agricultural projects, for example irrigation systems,
4. dispense with prestige objects like sports stadiums and conference halls,
5. encourage labour-intensive industry and the use of simple machinery,

monocultural [ˌmɒnəʊˈkʌltʃərəl] **farming**	Anbau in Monokultur
cash crop	für den Verkauf bestimmte Anbaufrucht
cocoa [ˈkəʊkəʊ]	Kakao
soybeans	Sojabohnen
self-sufficient economy	Selbstversorgungswirtschaft
sorghum/millet	Hirsearten
fertilizer	Dünger
pesticide	Schädlingsbekämpfungsmittel
insecticide	Insektenvertilgungsmittel
disinfectant	Desinfektionsmittel
locust [ˈləʊkəst] **infestation**	Heuschreckenplage
pest	*hier:* Schädling
to exploit	ausbeuten
to refine	veredeln
to process	weiterverarbeiten
finished product	Fertigprodukt
barrier [ˈbærɪə]	Schranke
waste	Verschwendung
affluence [ˈæflʊəns]	Überfluß, Reichtum
aid to developing countries	Entwicklungshilfe
family planning	Familienplanung
GNP (g ross n ational p roduct) [grəʊs]	Bruttosozialprodukt
preference [ˈprefərəns]	Vorzug
large-scale	groß(angelegt), Groß-
irrigation	Bewässerung
to dispense with	verzichten auf, ohne … auskommen
prestige [preˈstiːʒ]	Prestige-
labour-intensive [-ɪnˈtensɪv]	arbeitsintensiv

6. remove import barriers on Third-World products,
7. improve loan conditions for the poorest countries,
8. teach the people to read and write and give them more vocational training and technical assistance,
9. spend a higher percentage of the money donated to large aid organizations like the Red Cross, UNICEF, Oxfam, Save the Children Fund etc. on self-help projects, which enable people in the Third World to learn to help themselves.

to remove	abschaffen, beseitigen
loan conditions	Kreditbedingungen
vocational training	Berufsausbildung
technical assistance	technische Hilfe
to donate	spenden
UNICEF	UNICEF (United Nations Children's Fund)

Minorities

Native Americans – Basic information:

The Indians are the native people/inhabitants of North America; they were there long before Columbus 'discovered' America in 1492. Today there are about 1.6 million Native Americans in the USA (0.6 per cent of the entire population).

Diseases, tribal warfare and the conflict between whites and Indians have decimated the indigenous population, but, because of a high birth rate, their number is now growing again.

About half of the nearly 300 Native American tribes live on federal reservations mostly west of the Mississippi. Almost half of the Native Americans have moved to urban areas (Los Angeles has an Indian population of about 70,000) in the last few decades, but today many Indians unable to find work in the big cities return to the reservations despite the high unemployment rate awaiting them there, too.

Big US companies want to exploit the rich natural and mineral resources on the reservations (like coal, oil or uranium). Although Mother Earth is

native	eingeboren, ursprünglich
to decimate	stark schwächen, dezimieren
indigenous [ɪn'dɪdʒɪnəs]	einheimisch
tribe	Stamm
federal	Bundes-
reservation	Reservat
urban	städtisch
to exploit	ausbeuten
mineral resources	Bodenschätze

sacred to most Native Americans, some are willing to co-operate with these companies in return for a fair share of the profits made.

On the reservations today there are many tribal councils, which run their own communities, schools, police forces, job programs, housing and social services as well as agricultural and natural resource development. An American Indian Movement (AIM) has been founded to fight for more rights for the Indian tribes. It does not support the kind of political radicalism prevalent in the 1960s or 70s ('Red Power'), but tries to help Indian people to adjust to US society without losing too much of their spiritual heritage, their cultural identity and their distinctive way of life.

Indian protest:

1. We were dispossessed of much of our land in the 19th century, deprived of our landholdings and cultural heritage and driven from our tribal homelands by the white usurpers; we have been granted no right to self-determination.
2. Our traditional religion was suppressed by Christianization.
3. Large numbers of Indians – not only in the big cities but also on the reservations – are unemployed and poor. We depend too much on federal money for jobs, welfare, health care etc.; what will happen when severe budget cuts decimate these already meagrely funded government programs?
4. We have often received unfair treatment from the whites; many treaties have been broken by them; today we continue to fight for our rights.
5. We want to become independent and self-supporting by operating our own businesses (by exploiting oil, gas, coal, uranium, other minerals and timber).
6. The American education system wants us to assimilate our Indian culture to the dominant white culture.
7. But we have a unique position as American Indians and a right to self-determination; the whites must respect our cultural diversity.

The Aboriginals – Basic information:

The Aboriginals are the indigenous people, the original inhabitants, of Australia (they have been there for at least twenty thousand years). They are a tiny minority, constituting about one per cent of the Australian population (approximately 160,000 Aborigines).

sacred ['seɪkrɪd]	heilig
tribal council	Stammesrat
to run	*hier:* leiten
community	Gemeinschaft
housing services	Wohnberatung
prevalent ['prevələnt]	vorherrschend
to adjust	anpassen
spiritual heritage ['herɪtɪdʒ]	geistiges Erbe
cultural identity	kulturelle Eigenheit
distinctive	charakteristisch

to dispossess of	berauben
to deprive of	berauben
landholding	Landbesitz
tribal homeland	Stammesgebiet
usurper [ju:'zɜ:pə]	Eindringling
self-determination	Selbstbestimmung
to suppress	unterdrücken
Christianization	Bekehrung zum Christentum
welfare	Wohlfahrt, Sozialfürsorge
severe [sɪ'vɪə]	*hier:* einschneidend
budget ['bʌdʒɪt] **cuts**	Haushaltskürzungen
meagrely funded	mit geringen Geldmitteln ausgestattet
treaty	Vertrag
self-supporting	unabhängig, autark
timber	Holz
to assimilate [ə'sɪmɪleɪt]	(sich) anpassen
unique [ju'ni:k]	einzigartig
diversity [daɪ'vɜ:sətɪ]	Verschiedenheit

the Aboriginals [ˌæbə'rɪdʒənəlz], **Aborigines**	die Ureinwohner Australiens

The traditional way of life of the Aboriginals – living in groups of 20 to 50 people, observing age-old traditions and natural religions and surviving in the mainly dry regions as hunter-gatherers – has more or less been brought to an end in the last two centuries since Australia was discovered and subsequently settled by immigrants from Europe and elsewhere.

Today most Aboriginals live in missions and settlements on outback reserves (there are more than 350 separate reserves), or in urban areas. Many tradition-orientated family groups have moved to small, isolated outstations, where they live off the land.

They still have access to medical and educational facilities, food and goods from the central settlements, yet are freed from the 'pressures' exerted by the white advisers and large-scale communal life on reserves.

In the big cities community-welfare projects have been developed for the Aboriginals: they offer housing, health, legal and other services. The Aboriginals are now seeking to establish their own racial image and identity and to preserve as much as they can of their life-styles, beliefs, customs and traditions.

Aboriginal protest:

1. White immigrants have taken our land and we have lost our sovereignty. No just treaty has been made between the white government and our people.
2. Australia is dominated by white people and we blacks are discriminated against. White society is racially biased/ prejudiced: we do not, for example, receive fair treatment in trials.
3. The whites have destroyed our sense of identity, our community life and our traditional life-styles.
4. We are closer to nature and closer to authentic humanity; we primeval people have a wisdom that the whites have lost.
5. We do not want to have anything to do with white civilization and the high-tech society; nor do we wish to be assimilated, as assimilation would only lead to our extinction.
6. We demand the power to assert our land rights by laying claim to our traditional lands and we demand the power/right to stop mining (for uranium or bauxite, for example) on our land, to control tourism and to protect our sacred sites.
7. We must maintain our identity in the face of hostility, ignorance and exploitation.

to observe	*hier:* beachten
hunter-gatherer	Jäger und Sammler
mission	Missionsstation
settlement	Siedlung
outback	der australische Busch, Hinterland
reserve	Reservat
outstation	Außenstation
to live off	sich ernähren von
facilities	*hier:* Einrichtungen
adviser	Berater/in
large-scale	umfangreich, ausgedehnt
communal	Gemeinschafts-
community-welfare project	Sozialprogramm
to preserve	erhalten
sovereignty ['sɒvrəntɪ]	Eigenständigkeit
to discriminate against	benachteiligen, diskriminieren
biased ['baɪəst]	voreingenommen
prejudiced ['predʒʊdɪst]	voreingenommen
trial	Prozeß (vor Gericht)
authentic [ɔ:'θentɪk]	echt
humanity	Menschlichkeit
primeval [praɪ'mi:vl]	urzeitlich, Ur-
high-tech [-tek]	hochtechnisiert
extinction	Vernichtung, Ausrottung
to assert	*hier:* durchsetzen
sacred site ['seɪkrɪd]	heilige Stätte
hostility	Feindseligkeit
ignorance	Unwissenheit
exploitation	Ausbeutung

Serious problems of both minorities:

1. In general they are less healthy, poorer, and less well-educated than the rest of the population.
2. The lack of job opportunities leads to widespread unemployment,
3. inadequate housing,
4. alcohol abuse and drug addiction,
5. a higher infant mortality rate than the whites,
6. a lower life expectancy,
7. widespread discontentment, frustration, disease, malnutrition, depression and apathy.

housing	*hier:* Wohnverhältnisse
abuse [ə'bju:s]	Mißbrauch
drug addiction	Drogenabhängigkeit
infant mortality	Säuglingssterblichkeit
life expectancy	Lebenserwartung
discontentment	Unzufriedenheit
malnutrition [ˌmælnju:'trɪʃən]	Unterernährung
depression	Niedergeschlagenheit
apathy ['æpəθɪ]	Teilnahmslosigkeit

Mass Media: The Press

Basic information:

Britain is a nation of avid newspaper readers. More than 16 million people buy a copy of a morning paper and countless Britons spend part of every Sunday with the latest issue of their favourite Sunday paper. As there is keen competition between the mass circulation dailies and weeklies, reporters are constantly in search of scoops to raise their circulation figures.

Britain's newspaper market is very differentiated. In addition to the national Sundays (The Sunday Times, Sunday Telegraph, News of the World, etc.) there are five national 'quality' dailies and seven national 'popular' dailies (the latter are called tabloids). The quality newspapers, which are serious in content and approach and large in size, appeal chiefly to the educated classes, whereas the smaller tabloids with their many photos and striking headlines cater mainly for the less intellectual 'man or woman in the street'. Besides all these national papers there are many local dailies as well as weekly and monthly magazines and journals.

avid ['ævɪd]	eifrig
copy	Exemplar
issue ['ɪʃju:]	*hier:* Ausgabe
mass circulation	… mit sehr hoher Auflage
daily	Tageszeitung
weekly	Wochenzeitung
scoop	Exklusiv-, Erstmeldung, Knüller
circulation figures	Auflage(nhöhe)
quality (paper)	seriös(e Zeitung)
popular (paper)	Massenblatt, Boulevardzeitung
tabloid ['tæblɔɪd]	(kleinformatige) Boulevardzeitung
approach	Methode der Behandlung
headline	Schlagzeile
magazine [ˌmægə'zi:n]	Zeitschrift, Magazin
journal ['dʒɜ:nəl]	Zeitschrift

The quality papers	average circulation	political viewpoint
The Daily Telegraph	1,113,000	conservative
The Guardian	439,000	liberal/left of centre
The Times	441,000	right of centre
The Independent	405,000	middle of the road
The Financial Times	199,000	middle of the road

(average circulation figures from 1989)

Some of the down-market tabloids are The Sun, The Daily Mirror, The Daily Mail, The Daily Express etc., all of which have millions of readers.

To remain competitive, tabloids often entice readers with shocking and sensational stories, lurid details of scandals and crimes, pin-ups etc., which explains why they are sometimes called the 'gutter press' or 'yellow press'. Serious papers try to maintain a balance between the freedom of the press and the public's 'right to know' on the one hand and the journalistic code of ethics and the individual's right to privacy on the other.

In the USA there is no newspaper that, strictly speaking, can be defined as a national paper. Only The New York Times, The Washington Post, USA Today and The Wall Street Journal are of nation-wide importance. However, there are numerous local and regional papers as well as a wide variety of periodicals and news magazines (Time, Newsweek) etc.

In both Britain and the USA the press has undergone radical changes over the last few decades. As more and more small papers were bought up by powerful publishers, huge newspaper chains emerged: a trend towards concentration typical not only of the press but of the mass media in general. Another trend which has had a great impact on newspapers is that of syndication. Syndicated columns, cartoons etc. by prominent journalists and cartoonists are published by many different newspapers. Thanks to such news-reporting services as Reuter's and AP (Associated Press) the collection of information and coverage of foreign news have become more efficient. More recently, new techniques have replaced the traditional typesetters and printing presses.

Apart from some minor differences serious newspapers basically offer the same things: journalists cover events of national and international importance on the front page or back page, columnists write fashion, motoring or financial columns, there are special features on topics like education and gardening, sports reporters inform the readers on the sports pages, cartoonists amuse them with comic strips and cartoons and critics write reviews of the latest plays, books etc.

liberal ['lɪbərəl]	liberal
middle of the road	politisch gemäßigt
down-market *adj*	an die 'unteren Schichten' gerichtet
competitive [kəm'petətɪv]	konkurrenzfähig
to entice	anlocken
sensational	sensationell, groß aufgemacht
lurid [ljʊərɪd]	entsetzlich
pin-up	Foto einer (halb)nackten Frau
'gutter press'	Schmutzpresse
'yellow press'	Boulevardpresse
freedom of the press	Pressefreiheit
'right to know'	Recht auf Information
code of ethics	Sittenkodex
privacy ['prɪvəsɪ]	Privatsphäre
periodical [ˌpɪərɪ'ɒdɪkl]	Zeitschrift
news magazine	Nachrichtenmagazin
publisher	Verleger/in
syndication	Veröffentlichung in mehreren Zeitungen zugleich
column ['kɒləm]	Spalte, *hier:* (Meinungs)Beitrag
cartoon	Karikatur
cartoonist	Karikaturist/in
news-reporting services	Presse-/Nachrichtenagentur
coverage ['kʌvərɪdʒ]	Berichterstattung
technique [tek'ni:k]	Technik
typesetter	Schriftsetzer/in; Setzmaschine
printing press	Druckerpresse
to cover	berichten über
columnist ['kɒləmnɪst]	Feuilletonist/in, Leitartikler/in
feature	*hier:* spezieller Artikel
critic	Kritiker/in, Rezensent/in
review	Kritik, Rezension

Additional features are leading articles (leaders) written by the editor, correspondence columns with 'letters to the editor', the latest instalment of a serialized novel, notices of births, deaths and marriages, crossword puzzles, horoscopes and 'situations vacant' and 'situations wanted' advertisements. Considerable space is devoted to ads of various kinds, including classified ads, as newspapers could not survive without advertising revenues.

The publishing house has its papers printed and then taken to the newsagents. Subscribers' papers are delivered to their homes, as their subscription includes this service.

leading article (leader)	Leitartikel
editor (in chief)	Chefredakteur/in
letter to the editor	Leserbrief
instalment [ɪn'stɔ:lmənt]	*hier:* Fortsetzung
to serialize ['sɪərɪəlaɪz]	in Fortsetzungen veröffentlichen
notice	*hier:* Anzeige, Annonce
crossword puzzle ['pʌzl]	Kreuzworträtsel
'situations vacant' advertisement [əd'vɜ:tɪsmənt]	Stellenangebot, -anzeige
'situations wanted' advertisement	Stellengesuch
ad(vertisement)	Anzeige, Inserat, Annonce
classified ad	Kleinanzeige
advertising ['ædvətaɪsɪŋ] **revenues** ['revənju:z]	Einkünfte durch Werbung und Anzeigen
publishing house	Verlagshaus
newsagent ['nju:zeɪdʒənt]	Zeitungshändler/in
subscriber [səb'skraɪbə]	Abonnent/in
subscription	Abonnement

Mass Media: Radio and TV

Basic information:

If you want to listen to the radio, you switch on your radio set and tune in to a broadcasting station. You need an aerial *(BE)*/ antenna *(AE)*, a receiver, an amplifier and loudspeakers to receive good stereo quality on VHF (*AE:* FM). You can listen to the news and the weather forecast, to pop(ular) songs or classical music, to radio plays or to live broadcasts of sporting events, depending on what your favourite programmes are.

The BBC, which used to have a complete monopoly of radio and television broadcasting, has always been financed by annual payments/ licence fees. Though under government control, the BBC has full autonomy in choosing the content of its programmes and in running its own affairs.

ITV and the television programmes it broadcasts by private companies are financed by commercial advertising only.

There are also many private and independent local radio stations, which are financed by companies paying to have commercials, i.e. advertisements for their products, broadcast on the radio. Sometimes advertisers even sponsor their own programmes, e.g. a quiz show or a serial.

In addition to the thousands of local radio stations in the USA, there are three national networks – CBS, NBC and ABC – which dominate the radio services. Being the largest TV companies in the country, these three networks are also responsible for the majority of TV programmes broadcast nation-wide.

Cable TV and satellite TV

Cable TV, which was first introduced in the US, began to make its appearance in many European countries in the 1970s and 1980s. The deregulation of broadcasting in some countries led to the introduction of many private networks and satellites were launched, beaming station programmes into cable networks.

At first cable TV developed relatively slowly in most countries. There was one major problem: the cost of digging the roads up and of installing cables in people's homes. But the network is growing.

set	Gerät
to tune in to	(Sender, Programm) einstellen
broadcasting station	Sender
aerial ['eərɪəl]/**antenna**	Antenne
receiver	Empfänger
amplifier	Verstärker
VHF (very high frequency), FM (frequency modulation)	UKW
radio play	Hörspiel
live broadcast	Direktübertragung
programme	Programm, Sendung
BBC	(British Broadcasting Corporation)
monopoly [mə'nɒpəlɪ]	Monopol
licence fee	Lizenzgebühr
autonomy [ɔ:'tɒnəmɪ]	Selbständigkeit, Autonomie
ITV (Independent Television)	unabhängige, private Fernsehgesellschaft in GB
to broadcast	senden
commercial *(adj)*	kommerziell
advertising ['ædvətaɪzɪŋ]	Werbung
commercial *(n)*	Reklamesendung, Werbespot
advertisement [əd'vɜ:tɪsmənt]	Reklame, Werbung
advertiser ['ædvətaɪzə]	Werbeträger
to sponsor	unterstützen, fördern, *hier:* finanzieren
quiz show	Quizsendung
serial ['sɪərɪəl]	Serie, Sendereihe
network	Netz, Rundfunk- und Fernsehgesellschaft
deregulation	Liberalisierung, Aufhebung einschränkender Bestimmungen
to launch	starten
to beam	ausstrahlen
to install	*hier:* verlegen

Direct broadcasting by satellite is to be introduced in the 1990s, when there will be dozens of new (satellite) channels in addition to the ones already existing. Many countries in Europe have set up their own satellite broadcasting and all over the world private companies and government organizations plan to put more satellites into orbit.

An Example of commercial TV

British Sky Broadcasting, formerly known as Sky Channel, is a private British company. Launched in 1982 as a pan-European English-language entertainment satellite service, it is the pioneer satellite-to-cable channel in Europe and it now broadcasts to millions of cable-TV viewers in Europe. Its different channels can also be received directly via satellite if you have a dish aerial and a suitable TV set.

Its programmes are typical of private TV stations: panel games, family and variety shows, children's features, sitcoms, animated cartoons, westerns and thrillers (often imported US series), sport and music; in short, for the most part light entertainment.

Problems of TV today and in the future:

1. Twenty, or even as many as 40, programmes may be enough for most viewers: saturation point may have been reached.
2. Will competition between the TV stations lead to an improvement in the programmes of public-sector broadcasters like the BBC or does a larger number of channels inevitably lower the standards of all TV programmes?
3. More channels do not necessarily mean a wider spectrum for viewers: more variety may be offered by three state-run TV stations than by 30 private channels.
4. Trivialized and unbalanced news coverage must be avoided.
5. Will there be enough programmes for minorities, enough educational and arts programmes etc.?
6. Will satellite and cable TV alter viewing patterns, so that people will spend more time watching TV?
7. In order to protect young viewers from violent or pornographic programmes a legal framework and electronic devices in the TV sets are essential; it is a matter of parental control to ensure that children do not have access to such movies on video cassettes.

channel	Kanal
orbit	Umlaufbahn
pan- [pæn]	gesamt-
pioneer	wegbereitend
via ['vaɪə]	über, via
dish aerial	Parabolantenne
panel game	Ratespiel, Quiz
variety [və'raɪətɪ] **show**	Varieté(vorstellung)
feature	*hier:* Film
sitcom (situation comedy)	Situationskomödie
animated cartoon	Zeichentrickfilm
series ['sɪəri:z]	Serie
light entertainment	leichte Unterhaltung
viewer	Fernsehzuschauer/in
saturation point	Sättigungspunkt, -grad
competition	Wettbewerb
public-sector broadcaster	öffentlich-rechtliche Fernsehanstalt
to lower	senken
spectrum	Skala, Spektrum
variety [və'raɪətɪ]	Vielfalt
to trivialize	bagatellisieren
unbalanced	unausgewogen
coverage ['kʌvərɪdʒ]	Berichterstattung
arts	Kunst
to alter ['ɔ:ltə]	verändern
viewing pattern	Sehgewohnheit
framework	Rahmen
device	Vorrichtung
to ensure [ɪn'ʃʊə]	sicherstellen, sichergehen

A computer-dominated world

The high-tech revolution

Hackers – the new techno-terrorists

Is data protection possible?

Computers

Basic information:

Computing is commonly practised today and in nearly all spheres of life computerization is on the increase. Computers, mostly PCs, can be found in millions of homes and every major firm makes use of microcomputers, minicomputers and even, in some cases, mainframes. All these computers store, process and retrieve large amounts of data, but they differ in size, memory capacity and speed.

Computers are used in data-processing departments in business, industry, modern medicine, space exploration and by public authorities – the police, schools, traffic control etc. There is a wide range of applications, for example word processing, stock control, spreadsheet and chemical analysis.

An increasing number of people have begun to work from home, using a computer and a telephone modem. Today the software is more user friendly, the hardware more compact. More and more book-sized PCs – so-called laptop computers – are being produced. Although computers are time-saving, it takes a while to learn how to work with them: a special programming language is required (e.g. BASIC, PASCAL or ASSSEMBLER).

All computers have a central processing unit (CPU), which processes the data fed into it. A computer does not use digits like 1, 2 or 3 for its calculations, but only the two 'symbols' or binary digits 0 and 1, the so-called bits. The system is called the binary system: a binary number normally consists of eight bits, for example the number one is 0000 0001, number two 0000 0010 and number three 0000 0011 in the binary code. This combination of eight bits is called one byte.

high-tech [-tek]	hochtechnologisch
hacker	jemand, der sich illegal Zugang zu anderen Computersystemen verschafft
data ['deɪtə] **protection**	Datenschutz
to compute	rechnen, *hier:* Daten verarbeiten
computerization	Umstellung auf Computer
PC (personal computer)	Mikrocomputer, PC
microcomputer ['maɪkrəʊ-]	Mikrorechner, Mikrocomputer
mainframe	Großrechner
to store	speichern
to process	verarbeiten
to retrieve	*hier:* abrufen
memory capacity	Speicherkapazität
data processing	Datenverarbeitung
word processing	Textverarbeitung
stock control	Lager(bestands)führung
spreadsheet analysis [ə'næləsɪs]	Tabellenkalkulation
modem ['məʊdem]	Datenübertragungsgerät, Modem
software	Software (z. B. Programme)
user friendly	benutzerfreundlich
hardware	Hardware (die mechanischen u. elektronischen Teile eines Computers)
lap	Schoß
programming language	Programmiersprache
central processing unit (CPU)	Zentraleinheit
to feed	*hier:* eingeben
calculation	Rechnung
binary ['baɪnərɪ]	aus zwei Einheiten bestehend, binär
bit [bɪt]	Bit
byte [baɪt]	Byte

How a large computer works:

- to enter/gain access to the system, a code/password is required, which can be typed into the computer on the keyboard,
- a command is inserted and the data is entered into the computer from a keyboard, tape or floppy disc/disk (= input),
- the microprocessor in the computer performs the logical analyses or the arithmetical calculations,
- data is stored in the computer's memory system,
- the result of the analyses and calculations (= output) can be printed on paper by the printer, shown in the form of graphics on the monitor (or VDU) and can be stored on tapes, disks etc.

A computer simply follows instructions. No computer can produce useful results if the information/data put into the computer or programme is inferior or incomplete. In other words, GIGO = Garbage In – Garbage Out.

Hacking:

A hacker who wants to invade sophisticated data networks illegally

- calls up a programme,
- breaks into a system by using other people's passwords,
- may even delete a system by means of this kind of electronic infiltration: a 'virus' (a destructive programme) that can wipe out a computer's data files may be planted deliberately.

As a result, various antiviral programmes have been invented to detect and delete the viruses.

General dangers:

- The linking of information from every source available may make it possible to form a complete and accurate picture of every citizen. People may thus become 'transparent' (der 'gläserne Mensch').
- A threat to privacy is constituted by the growth of data banks etc. Total control over human beings is no longer inconceivable.
- Misuse of data or data manipulation is possible: data protection may become more and more difficult, even impossible, to guarantee and supervise.

code	Codewort
password	Kennwort
keyboard	Tastatur
command	Befehl
to insert	eingeben
tape	Band
floppy disc *(BE)*/**disk** *(AE)*	Diskette
input	(Daten-, Programm-)Eingabe
microprocessor	Mikroprozessor
analysis [-sɪs], *pl* **analyses** [ə'næləsi:z]	Analyse(n)
output	(Daten-)Ausgabe
printer	Drucker
graphics	graphische Darstellungen
monitor	Bildschirm, Monitor
VDU (visual display unit)	Bildschirm, Monitor
instruction	Anweisung
inferior	minderwertig, fehlerhaft
garbage	Müll, *hier:* wertlose Daten
sophisticated	hochentwickelt
network	Netz
to delete	tilgen, löschen
infiltration	Eindringen
virus ['vaɪərəs]	Virus
data file	Datei
deliberately [dɪ'lɪbərɪtlɪ]	absichtlich
to detect	aufspüren
source	Quelle
privacy ['prɪvəsɪ]	Privatsphäre
data bank	Datenbank
inconceivable [ˌɪnkən'si:vəbl]	unvorstellbar
misuse	Mißbrauch
to supervise	überwachen

Space

Basic information:

Space exploration started in 1957 with the launching of the Russian satellite 'Sputnik I'. Manned space travel followed when a Russian cosmonaut was the first to orbit the earth. The Apollo moon landing, a soft landing and subsequent re-launch, was accomplished by American astronauts in 1969. Further developments include the space shuttle and permanent space stations.

While unmanned space probes continue to explore deep space, the main interest now is in communications satellites and meteorological satellites (which are usually in a geostationary position), in spy satellites and manned space stations or laboratories. They are used for research as they allow experiments under conditions of weightlessness or zero gravity.

"You have a go in ours, and we'll have a go in yours, okay?"

exploration	Erforschung
to launch	starten
satellite ['sætəlaɪt]	Satellit
(un-)manned	(un-)bemannt
cosmonaut ['kɒzmənɔːt]	russisches Wort für Astronaut/in
to orbit	umkreisen
moon landing	Mondlandung
re-launch	erneuter Start
astronaut ['æstrənɔːt]	Astronaut/in
space station	Raumstation
probe	Sonde
deep space	die Tiefe des Weltalls
communications	Nachrichten-
meteorological [ˌmiːtɪərə'lɒdʒɪkl]	Wetter-
geostationary [ˌdʒiːəʊ'steɪʃənərɪ]	an einem festen Punkt über der Erde
spy	Spionage-
laboratory [lə'bɒrətrɪ]	Labor
research	Forschung
weightlessness	Schwerelosigkeit
zero gravity [-'grævətɪ]	(Zustand der) Schwerelosigkeit

The launching of a rocket:

Orbiters, shuttles, space stations and satellites are the payload of a carrier rocket, which sits on a launch(ing) pad at a launching site.

During the countdown all systems are constantly checked, mainly by computers. If no system failures or other flaws are detected, the countdown runs to three – two – one – zero – ignition (and lift-off). Once the spacecraft has reached a certain altitude, the (normally two) booster rocket stages are jettisoned, as well as the external fuel tank. When in orbit, the shuttle's onboard computers control its steering and navigation – its own orbital manoeuvring system takes over.

A space shuttle, consisting of the orbiter (as part of the payload), the external fuel tank and the solid-fuel booster rockets, places satellites in orbit or docks modules on to a space station. It may deliver supplies or be used to exchange crew members.

The return to earth:

The space shuttle, which is protected by heat-resistant tiles during its re-entry into the earth's atmosphere, can land on any airstrip or runway. Great progress has been made since the Apollo space missions, when the capsules splashed down in the ocean by parachute and were picked up by a ship.

orbiter	Satellit
(space) shuttle	Raumfähre
payload	Nutzlast
carrier rocket	Trägerrakete
launch(ing) pad	Abschußrampe
launching site	Abschußbasis
to check	überprüfen
failure ['feɪljə]	*hier:* Störung, Defekt
flaw	Fehler
ignition	Zündung
lift-off	Start
spacecraft	Raumschiff
altitude ['æltɪtju:d]	Höhe
booster rocket	Antriebsrakete
stage	Stufe
to jettison	abwerfen
external fuel tank	äußerer Treibstofftank
to steer	steuern
manoeuvring [mə'nu:vrɪŋ] **system**	Steuerungssystem
solid fuel	Festbrennstoff
to dock	anlegen, ankoppeln
module ['mɒdju:l]	*hier:* Kapsel
supply	Nachschub
crew	Mannschaft

heat-resistant tile	hitzebeständige Keramikplatte
re-entry	Wiedereintritt
airstrip	(Behelfs)Landeplatz
runway	Start-, Landebahn
mission	Einsatz, Mission
capsule ['kæpsju:l]	Kapsel
to splash down	im Wasser landen
parachute ['pærəʃu:t]	Fallschirm

A new breed: half sheep, half goat

Embryo donation and preservation

Genetic therapy may cure heart disease

The cloning of human beings

Is the future of the human species at risk?

Genetic Engineering

Basic information:

Every living creature contains more than 100,000 genes, which are the units in chromosomes controlling heredity. The genes are made of DNA, the hereditary material (the 'building bricks'), which contains the genetic code of a living being; it is by this material that its cellular structure is defined.

Many people have inherited diseases because of a defect in just one of their genes. In Britain, for example, about one in 500 people suffers from a hereditary form of heart disease. Some of their children can be helped by gene replacement therapy, by gene transplants before birth (defective genes are replaced by sound ones). Human gene transplants may soon be a common practice in laboratories.

Genetic engineering, like biotechnology in general, is a new science. It poses incalculable risks and many moral and ethical questions (for example, the artificial creation and cloning of human beings). On the other hand, it can be beneficial to modern medicine: certain diseases which cause misery, pain and distress to both children and parents can be eradicated in this way.

breed	Züchtung, Rasse
goat	Ziege
embryo donation	Spenden von Embryos
preservation	Erhaltung, Konservierung
genetic therapy ['θerəpɪ]	Gen-Behandlung
cloning ['kləʊnɪŋ]	Schaffung von erbgleichen Wesen
species ['spi:ʃi:z]	Art, Gattung

genetic engineering [dʒɪ'netɪk-]	Gentechnik
living creature ['kri:tʃə]	Lebewesen
gene [dʒi:n]	Gen
chromosome ['krəʊmə,səʊm]	Chromosom
heredity [hɪ'redɪtɪ]	ererbte Anlagen, Erbmasse
DNA (deoxyribonucleic acid)	DNS
hereditary [hɪ'redɪtərɪ]	er-, vererbt
genetic code	genetischer Code
cellular structure	Zellstruktur
to inherit	erben
defect	Fehler, Defekt
replacement	Ersatz
transplant	Übertragung, Transplantation
laboratory [lə'bɒrətrɪ]	Labor
biotechnology [-tek'nɒlədʒɪ]	Biotechnologie
artificial creation	künstliche Erzeugung, Schöpfung
beneficial [,benɪ'fɪʃl]	nützlich, vorteilhaft
distress	Leid
to eradicate [ɪ'rædɪkeɪt]	ausrotten

Examples of applied genetic engineering:

1. Genetically engineered sheep produce human proteins to combat blood diseases, for example haemophilia B. The researchers inject human genes, which code the factor-IX protein, into the fertilized eggs of sheep so that the protein will finally emerge in the animal's milk, from which it must then be isolated.
2. Scientists have found a way of correcting a hereditary defect which causes a severe form of heart disease (people who inherit this disease suffer from high cholesterol levels). They have inserted a gene that controls body cholesterol levels into liver cells, using a specially created virus. So far this technique has worked in rabbit cells.

Geneticists' arguments for genetic engineering:

1. By producing hybrids of plants (for example hybrid wheat) or animals (half sheep, half goat) they can help farmers worldwide: grain grows faster and is made resistant to insects and diseases; animals are more productive, need less food etc.
2. Hybrid animals can produce drugs and help modern medicine in its search for new products to combat blood diseases etc.
3. Through modification of an embryo's structure at an early stage some genetic risks can be excluded.
4. The discovery of a defective gene need not necessarily raise the option of abortion: preventive treatment may suffice.

Moral and ethical questions raised by genetic engineering:

1. The dignity of the unborn child, its uniqueness and specificity must be respected: the embryo's life ought to be protected from the moment of fertilization on.
2. Should certain types of experimentation on embryos be allowed in spite of the danger of human beings being regarded as laboratory material?
3. Should an embryo be aborted if it has a defective gene which has been discovered prenatally?
4. Scientists may attempt to produce a super-species of human being: they may use gene transplants to enhance physical appearance, talents or intelligence, which could give rise to the danger of genetic manipulation.

protein ['prəʊtiːn]	Protein
to combat ['kɒmbæt]	bekämpfen
haemophilia B [hiːməʊ'fɪlɪə]	Bluterkrankheit (Typ B)
researcher	Forscher/in
to inject	einspritzen, injizieren
to code	codieren
factor IX [naɪn]	Blutgerinnungsfaktor
to fertilize	befruchten
to emerge	erscheinen
scientist	(Natur)Wissenschaftler/in
cholesterol [kə'lestərɒl] **level**	Cholesterinspiegel
to insert	einsetzen
liver cell ['lɪvə]	Leberzelle
virus ['vaɪərəs]	Virus
technique [tek'niːk]	Technik, Verfahren, Methode
rabbit	Kaninchen
geneticist	Genetiker/in, Gentechniker/in
hybrid ['haɪbrɪd]	Kreuzung
plant	Pflanze
hybrid wheat	Hybridweizen
grain	Getreide
resistant	widerstandsfähig, resistent
drug	*hier:* Arznei
modification	Änderung
early stage	Frühstadium
option of abortion	Wahl/Möglichkeit einer Abtreibung
preventive treatment	*hier:* Vorsorgemaßnahmen
to suffice [sə'faɪs]	genügen

dignity	Würde
uniqueness [juː'niːknɪs]	Einzigartigkeit
specificity [ˌspesɪfɪsɪtɪ]	Besonderheit
experimentation on	Experimentieren mit/an
to abort	abtreiben
defective	fehlerhaft
prenatally [ˌpriː'neɪtəlɪ]	vor der Geburt
super-species ['spiːʃiːz]	Superrasse
to enhance [ɪn'hɑːns]	verbessern, steigern
physical appearance	äußeres Erscheinungsbild
genetic manipulation	Genmanipulation

Test-tube Babies and Surrogate Motherhood

Basic information:

Since the first test-tube baby was born in Britain in 1978, there have been thousands of such births and the number is on the increase. This method of artificial insemination is no longer as controversial as it was some years ago because both egg and sperm are taken from the parents.

The donor eggs are fertilized in the laboratory by sperm from the husband of the mother-to-be. Then the eggs are deep-frozen until the optimum moment in the recipient mother's natural cycle. Finally the egg, which has been fertilized in vitro, is transplanted into the uterus.

In 1985 the first birth of a baby born to a surrogate mother for money took place in Britain ('Baby Cotton'). There was a somewhat hostile reaction on the part of the public on moral and legal grounds: you 'buy' a baby that has yet to be conceived and you pay a woman to have a fertilized egg implanted and bear a baby that she will later have to give away.

It is now even possible to defrost human embryos and place them in surrogate mothers. As many childless couples long to have a baby, highly fertile women 'rich in eggs' donate ova to infertile women deficient in eggs: women willing to be egg donors give their surplus eggs to the hospital.

Moral, ethical and legal problems:

1. The egg donor's background must be probed into very carefully to ensure that she is not a drug addict, does not suffer from Aids etc.
2. Should embryos be implanted in childless women?
3. How long should surplus embryos be stored in 'embryo banks' (fertilized eggs can be successfully stored for some years) and what should be done with surplus embryos later in order to prevent possible abuse?
4. What if the baby is deformed?
5. How will the parents react if, instead of one baby, twins or triplets are born?
6. Should surrogate motherhood for financial gain be prohibited and infertile couples be encouraged to adopt children instead?

test-tube baby	im Reagenzglas gezeugtes Baby
surrogate ['sʌrəgɪt] **motherhood**	Leihmutterschaft

artificial [ˌaːtɪ'fɪʃl] **insemination**	künstliche Befruchtung
controversial [ˌkɒntrə'vɜːʃl]	umstritten
egg	Ei, Eizelle
sperm [spɜːm]	Samen
donor ['dəʊnə(r)]	Spender/in
to fertilize	befruchten
laboratory [lə'bɒrətrɪ]	Labor
mother-to-be	zukünftige Mutter
deep-frozen	tiefgefroren
recipient [rɪ'sɪpɪənt]	Empfänger/in
natural cycle	natürlicher Zyklus
in vitro [ˌɪn'viːtrəʊ]	im Reagenzglas
to transplant	verpflanzen, transplantieren
uterus ['juːtərəs]	Gebärmutter
surrogate mother	Leihmutter
to conceive	empfangen
to implant	einpflanzen
to bear a baby	ein Baby austragen
to defrost	auftauen
embryo ['embrɪəʊ]	Embryo
childless couple	kinderloses Ehepaar
fertile ['fɜːtaɪl]/**infertile**	fruchtbar/unfruchtbar
to donate [dəʊ'neɪt]	spenden
ovum *(sg)*, **ova** *(pl)*	Ei, Eizelle
surplus ['sɜːpləs]	*hier:* überzählig
drug addict	Drogensüchtige(r)
to store	lagern
abuse [ə'bjuːs]	Mißbrauch
deformed	mißgebildet
twins	Zwillinge
triplets ['trɪplɪts]	Drillinge
to adopt	adoptieren

Air Pollution – Acid Rain and the Dying Forests

Basic information:

Air pollution is one of the most serious problems of our day and age. A lot of damage has already been done to human health, forests and crops worldwide. There are many poisonous substances in the air, emitted by industry in general, coal- and oil-fired power stations, domestic coal fires, cars etc.

Countries throughout the Northern hemisphere have been adversely affected by air pollution in the last few decades. Central Europe, the Alpine region, Eastern Europe, Scandinavia and parts of the USA and Canada are hardest hit; Great Britain is slightly better off because the Atlantic winds 'export' most noxious fumes to the Continent.

Acid rain:

Rainwater becomes acidic when emissions like sulphur dioxide from factories and power stations and, to a lesser degree, the nitrogen oxides emitted by car exhausts are dissolved in it, so that acids, such as sulphuric acid, are produced in the atmosphere.

It has been proved that this acid rain is partly to blame for the 'Waldsterben', the irreparable damage done to Germany's many extensive forests.

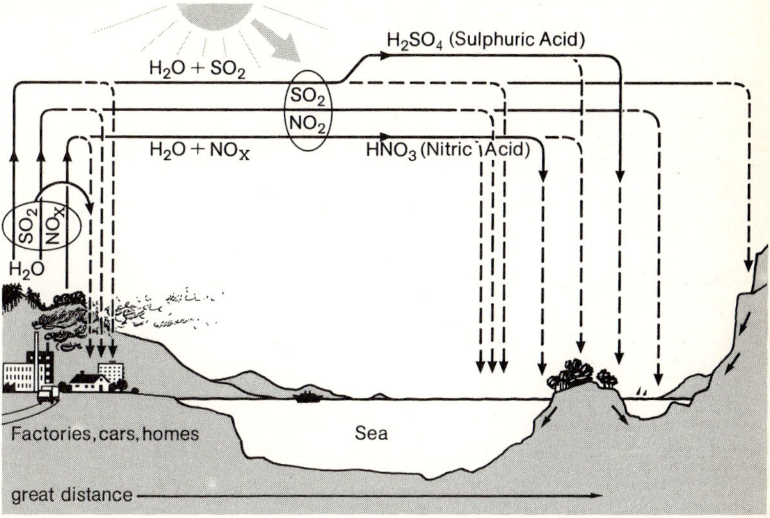

pollution	Verschmutzung
acid ['æsɪd] **rain**	saurer Regen
poisonous substance	giftiger Stoff
to emit	ausstoßen
power station	Kraftwerk
domestic coal fire	Hausbrand
hemisphere ['hemɪˌsfɪə]	Halbkugel
to affect	betreffen
hardest hit	am schlimmsten betroffen
noxious ['nɒkʃəs]	schädlich
fume	Dampf, Rauch

acidic [ə'sɪdɪk]	sauer
emission	Ausstoß
sulphur dioxide [daɪ'ɒksaɪd]	Schwefeldioxid
nitrogen oxides ['naɪtrədʒən]	Stickstoffoxide (NO_x)
to dissolve [dɪ'zɒlv]	(sich) auflösen
sulphuric [sʌl'fjʊərɪk] **acid**	Schwefelsäure
atmosphere ['ætməsfɪə]	Atmosphäre

Symptoms of dying trees:

1. The leaves or needles turn yellow.
2. Older leaves or needles die and fall off.
3. The growth of new shoots is stunted.
4. The twigs on the uppermost branches thin out.
5. Crown density is reduced.
6. Branches go limp.

Other effects of acid rain:

1. Fish and plants in many lakes, rivers and streams have died.
2. Health problems: respiratory disorders such as asthma, bronchitis etc.
3. 'High stacks' policy: pollution in the immediate vicinity of power stations is reduced, only to be spread further afield.
4. Damage to historic buildings: millions have to be spent on fighting erosion, on restoring stonework etc.
5. Damage limitation is a costly undertaking – the consumer must pay for a healthier environment.

How to fight air pollution:

1. make a global pact aimed at curtailing pollution worldwide,
2. make modifications in fossil-fuel-burning power stations, for example the installation of filters,
3. curb vehicle exhaust fumes emissions by encouraging the use of catalytic converters and unleaded petrol,
4. support the development of the lean-burn engine for cars, which improves fuel efficiency and thus produces fewer emissions,
5. introduce speed limits on motorways to reduce the output of carbon monoxide, oxides of nitrogen and hydrocarbons,
6. pass stricter laws to combat air pollution,
7. carry out more research into the potential use of alternative renewable sources of energy.

shoot	Trieb
to stunt	im Wachstum hemmen
twig	Zweig
to thin (out)	sich lichten
crown density	Kronendichte
to go limp	*hier:* herunterhängen

respiratory disorder ['respərətərɪ]	Erkrankung der Atemwege
asthma ['æsmə]	Asthma
bronchitis [brɒŋ'kaɪtɪs]	Bronchitis
'high stacks' policy	Politik der 'hohen Schornsteine'
vicinity [vɪ'sɪnɪtɪ]	Nachbarschaft
further afield	weiter weg
historic	historisch bedeutsam
to restore	wiederherstellen, restaurieren
stonework	Mauerwerk
damage limitation	Schadensbegrenzung
consumer	Verbraucher/in, Konsument/in
environment [ɪn'vaɪərənmənt]	Umwelt

to curtail [kɜː'teɪl]	begrenzen, eindämmen
modification	Änderung
fossil fuel	fossiler Brennstoff
to curb [kɜːb]	eindämmen, verringern
exhaust [ɪg'zɔːst]	Auspuff
fumes	Abgase
catalytic converter	Katalysator
unleaded [ʌn'ledɪd]	bleifrei
lean-burn engine	Magermotor
fuel efficiency	Energieeinsparung
carbon monoxide [mɒn'ɒksaɪd]	Kohlenmonoxid
hydrocarbon [ˌhaɪdrəʊ'kɑːbən]	Kohlenwasserstoff
to combat ['kɒmbæt]	bekämpfen
research	Forschung
renewable	erneuerbar
source of energy	Energiequelle

The Destruction of the Ozone Layer and the Greenhouse Effect

Basic information:

The destruction or depletion of the world's vital ozone layer may turn out to be the major environmental issue of the 21st century.

Ozone in the stratosphere is vital to life because it screens us from most of the sun's harmful radiation: it shields/protects the earth. It absorbs more than 99 per cent of the lethal ultraviolet rays reaching the earth's atmosphere. The ozone layer is created by the interaction of ultraviolet radiation from the sun with oxygen in the atmosphere. But, as a result of the decline in the ozone layer, there is an increase in the amount of ultraviolet light that reaches the earth, so that life on earth is now exposed to increasingly dangerous levels of radiation.

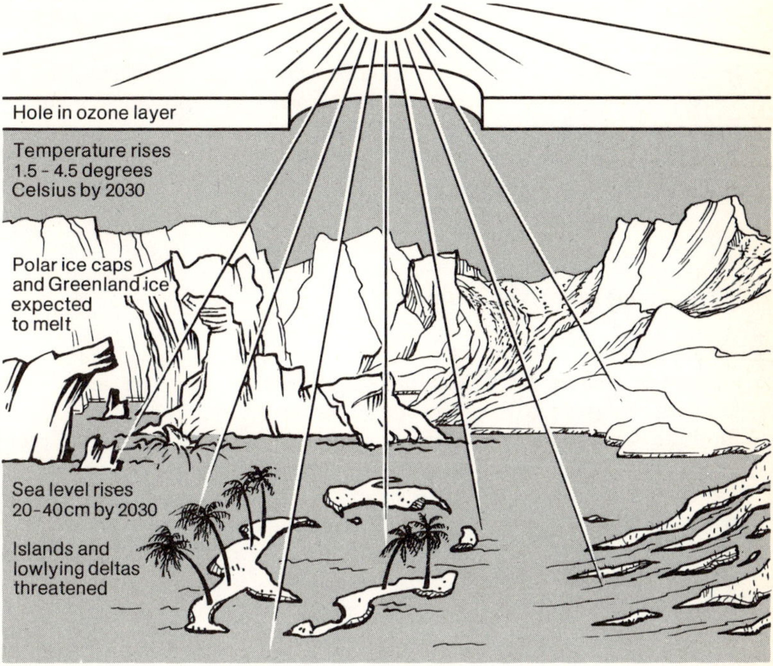

ozone layer ['əʊzəʊn 'leɪə]	Ozonschicht
greenhouse effect	Treibhauseffekt
depletion [dɪ'plɪ:ʃn]	Ausdünnung, Substanzverlust
issue ['ɪʃju:]	Streitfrage, Problem
stratosphere ['strætəʊsfɪə]	Stratosphäre
to screen from	abschirmen vor
harmful	schädlich
radiation	Strahlung
to shield	schützen
lethal ['li:θl]	tödlich
ray	Strahl
interaction	Wechselwirkung
ultraviolet [ˌʌltra'vaɪəlɪt]	ultraviolett, UV-
oxygen ['ɒksɪdʒən]	Sauerstoff
to be exposed to	ausgesetzt sein
level	*hier:* Grad

There is an indirect link between the damage to the ozone layer and the greenhouse effect, the overheating of the earth or global warming. Carbon dioxide (CO_2) and other greenhouse gases are accumulating in the atmosphere at an alarming pace. The increasing concentrations of greenhouse gases block the escape of infra-red radiation from the earth into space; they prevent the earth from reflecting solar heat back into space and trap it in the lower air.

The reasons for this phenomenon:

Scientists argue that the depletion of the ozone layer is caused mainly by man-made pollutants: CFCs, which propel aerosols, are also to be found in refrigerators (as refrigerants), insulation in houses, the foam in furniture and car seats, air-conditioners, solvents, some fast-food containers etc. At first harmless, they do not react until they have floated some 20 km up into the stratosphere. There they are broken down, giving off chlorine, and attack ozone molecules.

Man is also mainly to blame for the greenhouse effect, which can be traced back to fossil fuel combustion in vehicles, power stations, factories and homes, as well as to the large-scale burning of tropical forests.

The dangerous greenhouse gases are:

- carbon dioxide (CO_2) from fossil fuel combustion,
- nitrous oxides from nitrates used as fertilizers,
- methane (CH_4) from paddy fields and the bowels of cattle and sheep,
- chlorofluorocarbons (CFCs).

Possible consequences:

1. The rise in temperature may cause the polar ice caps to melt, which would lead to a rise in sea levels. One metre would be enough to flood many coastal regions.
2. Storms, droughts and heatwaves may cause destruction, famines etc.
3. The adverse effect on vegetation and crops may lead to widespread malnutrition and even starvation among animals and humans.
4. Drinking water may become scarce, reservoirs may dry up.

global warming	weltweite Erwärmung
carbon dioxide (CO_2) [daɪ'ɒksaɪd]	Kohlendioxid
to accumulate	sich ansammeln
infra-red	Infrarot-/Wärme-
to trap	*hier:* einschließen, festhalten

phenomenon [fɪ'nɒmɪnən]	Erscheinung, Phänomen
pollutant	Schadstoff
CFCs (chlorofluorocarbons)	FCKWs (Fluorchlorkohlenwasserstoffe)
to propel [prə'pel]	*hier:* als Treibmittel dienen für
aerosol ['eərəʊsɒl]	Spraydose
refrigerant	Kühlmittel
insulation	Isolierung
foam	Schaumstoff
solvent ['sɒlvənt]	Lösungsmittel
chlorine ['klɔ:ri:n]	Chlor
molecule ['mɒlɪkju:l]	Molekül
fossil fuel	fossiler Brennstoff
combustion	Verbrennung
nitrous oxides ['naɪtrəs]	Stickstoffoxide (NO_x)
nitrate ['naɪtreɪt]	Nitrat
methane ['mi:θeɪn]	Methan
paddy field	Reisfeld
bowels ['baʊəlz]	Eingeweide, Darm

sea level	Meeresspiegel
to flood [flʌd]	überfluten, überschwemmen
drought [draʊt]	Dürre
heatwave	Hitzewelle
famine ['fæmɪn]	Hungersnot
adverse	nachteilig
crop	Feldfrucht, Ernte(ergebnis)
malnutrition [ˌmælnju:'trɪʃən]	Unterernährung
starvation	Hungertod
reservoir ['rezəvwɑ:(r)]	Reservoir, Stausee
to dry up	austrocknen

5. With a change in rainfall patterns, land for farming may also be parched, which may result in soil erosion and in the desertification of formerly fertile areas.
6. More and more people may contract skin cancer and cataract.

Possible solutions to the problem:

1. Drastically phase out or prohibit the production of aerosol sprays and develop alternative compounds to replace CFCs.
2. Enforce tough controls on emissions to identify culprits and fine them.
3. Burn less coal or oil in order to reduce CO_2 emissions.
4. Make heating, lighting, domestic appliances and industrial machinery more energy-efficient; use energy-saving technologies.
5. Use better energy-conservation equipment in buildings.
6. Employ the huge quantities of waste heat from generators for heating buildings.
7. Develop new sources of energy not derived from fossil fuels (wind, water, tidal, geothermal and solar energy, i.e. renewable energy resources).

to parch	austrocknen
soil erosion	Bodenerosion
desertification [dɪˌzɜːtɪfɪˈkeɪʃən]	Versteppung, Wüstwerdung
fertile	fruchtbar
skin cancer	Hautkrebs
cataract [ˈkætərækt]	Grauer Star (Augenkrankheit)

compound	Verbindung
to enforce	*hier:* durchsetzen
emission	(Schadstoff)Ausstoß
culprit [ˈkʌlprɪt]	Sünder/in *hier:* Umweltsünder/in
to fine	mit einer Geldstrafe belegen
lighting	Beleuchtung
domestic appliance [-əˈplaɪəns]	Haushaltsgerät
energy-efficient	energiesparend
energy conservation	Energieeinsparung
waste heat	Abwärme
generator	Stromerzeuger, Generator
to derive from [dɪˈraɪv]	zurückführen auf, herleiten von
tidal	Gezeiten-
geothermal [ˌdʒiːəʊˈθɜːml]	… aus Erdwärme
solar energy	Sonnenenergie, Solarenergie
renewable	erneuerbar

Our oceans are polluted

Waters turned into garbage dumps

Higher nitrate levels in drinking water

Beaches closed

Is the ecosystem breaking down?

Water Pollution and the Waste Problem

Basic information:

Water pollution, which has become a problem worldwide, is one of the vital issues of our times. The coastal waters have suffered the worst effects of pollution as they have become the dumping ground for industrial waste. Dumping sewage and toxic waste – untreated – in the sea or on unlicensed dumps is quite a common practice, sometimes even the rule.

One reason for the increase in water pollution is overpopulation. Other reasons are inadequate waste management and waste disposal.

Thus large quantities of effluents containing heavy metals like lead, cadmium, zinc etc. are discharged into rivers or the coastal waters and towns and large cities have more and more sewage to dispose of. Seri-

garbage dump	Müllhalde
to dump	ablagern, abladen
nitrate ['naɪtreɪt] **level**	*hier:* Nitratgehalt

pollution	Verschmutzung
waste	Abfall, Müll
issue ['ɪʃju:]	Problem
coastal waters	Küstengewässer
dumping ground	Abladeplatz, Müllhalde
industrial waste	Industrieabfall
sewage ['sju:ɪdʒ]	Abwasser
toxic waste	Giftmüll
untreated	unbehandelt
unlicensed	nicht genehmigt
overpopulation	Überbevölkerung
inadequate [ɪn'ædɪkwət]	unzureichend
waste management	Abfallbeseitigung, -bewältigung
waste disposal	Abfallbeseitigung
effluent	Abwasser
heavy metal	Schwermetall
lead [led]	Blei
cadmium	Cadmium
zinc [zɪŋk]	Zink
to discharge	*hier:* ableiten
to dispose of	beseitigen, loswerden

ous problems are posed not only by the huge quantity but also by the kind of waste involved. Although most sewage-treatment plants are equipped to extract solids and organic matter from sewage, they are normally incapable of removing harmful and toxic chemical substances. Therefore synthetic detergents, heavy metals and dissolved phosphates and nitrates eventually end up in the sea.

Drinking water for millions of people has been contaminated by dangerous pollutants.

The immune systems of animals have been impaired by water pollution. In 1988 thousands of seals died in the North Sea, so that they were in danger of becoming extinct. Every year algae blooms (known as 'red tides') kill marine life in large areas. Survivors of decimated species are already afflicted with a number of symptoms: they have skin infections, their skeletons are deformed and they have developed tumours.

Ways of coping with water pollution and waste:

1. International co-operation and joint remedial action are necessary.
2. More and better sewage-treatment plants must be built.
3. The use of artificial fertilizers in agriculture must be reduced.
4. Sewage-sludge dumping in the sea must be prohibited.
5. As toxic chemicals leaking into the water supply can have long-term effects on human health, the burial of waste underground in storage tanks should be restricted.
6. Stricter laws for dealing with polluters must be passed and tougher controls enforced.
7. Consumers must be encouraged to cull their household garbage and industry to recycle the huge amounts of waste produced.
8. The general public must become aware of the ecological advantages of biodegradable substances over products which decompose either very slowly or not at all.
9. Waste prevention, i.e. keeping the production of waste to the absolute minimum, must become a common goal.

sewage-treatment plant	Kläranlage
solid ['sɒlɪd]	fester Stoff
detergent [dɪ'tɜ:dʒənt]	Reinigungsmittel, Waschmittel
to dissolve [dɪ'zɒlv]	auflösen
phosphate ['fɒsfeɪt]	Phosphat
to contaminate	verseuchen
pollutant	Schadstoff
immune system	Immunsystem
to impair	*hier:* schwächen
extinct	ausgestorben
algae bloom ['ældʒi: blu:m]	Algenblüte
marine [mə'ri:n] **life**	die Tierwelt des Meeres
to decimate	stark schwächen, dezimieren
skin infection	Infektionskrankheit der Haut
skeleton ['skelɪtən]	Skelett
deformed	verunstaltet, mißgebildet
tumo(u)r ['tju:mə]	Geschwulst, Tumor

to cope with	fertigwerden mit
joint	gemeinsam, solidarisch
remedial [rɪ'mi:djəl] **action**	Rettungsaktion
fertilizer	Dünger, Düngemittel
sewage-sludge dumping	Klärschlammverklappung
to leak	durchsickern
water supply	*hier:* Grundwasser
long-term effects	Langzeitwirkungen
polluter	Verschmutzer, Umweltsünder
to enforce	durchsetzen
to cull	auslesen
to recycle	wiederverwerten
biodegradable	biologisch abbaubar
to decompose	sich zersetzen
prevention	*hier:* Vermeidung
goal	Ziel

Drugs

Basic information:

When we speak about drugs, we normally mean the soft drugs marijuana and hash(ish) and hard drugs like heroin, cocaine or crack. But there are many more drugs available, like opium, LSD etc. Some are even used medically, for example morphine, amphetamines or barbiturates: only the continued abuse of such medical drugs is really dangerous.

Not only hard drugs but also soft drugs have harmful consequences for people's health. They are habit-forming and alter patterns of mood, thought and behaviour. No matter whether the drugs are taken as pills, smoked, snorted or injected intravenously, they will sooner or later lead to physical, psychic and mental dependence and consequently to addiction. Drugs cannot be taken in a moderate and controlled way over a long period because no drug is non-addictive. Once stronger doses of soft drugs are needed, the use of hard drugs often becomes inevitable.

soft drugs	weiche Drogen
marijuana [ˌmærɪ'hwɑːnə]	Marihuana
hash(ish) ['hæʃiːʃ]	Haschisch
hard drugs	harte Drogen
cocaine [kəʊ'keɪn]	Kokain
crack	Kokainderivat, Crack
available	verfügbar
morphine ['mɔːfiːn]	Morphium
amphetamine [æm'fetəmɪn]	Amphetamin, Aufputschmittel
barbiturate [bɑː'bɪtjʊrət]	Barbiturat, Schlafmittel
abuse [ə'bjuːs]	Mißbrauch
harmful	schädlich
habit-forming	süchtig machend
to alter ['ɔːltə]	verändern
to snort	schnupfen
to inject intravenously [ˌɪntrə'viːnəslɪ]	intravenös einspritzen
physical	körperlich, physisch
psychic ['saɪkɪk]	seelisch
mental	geistig
addiction	Sucht
moderate ['mɒdərət]	maßvoll
non-addictive	nicht süchtig machend
dose	Menge, Dosis

The drug-producing countries:

Peru, Bolivia, Colombia and Mexico are the main traditional producers of the coca-leaf and hemp/cannabis. Another large drug-producing region, which is the chief source of poppy seeds, is the 'Golden Triangle' in South-East Asia (Thailand, Burma and Laos), but the opium poppy is also grown in Pakistan and Afghanistan. In Northern Africa and the Middle East hashish is produced in large quantities.

However, the cultivation and production of drugs is no longer confined to Third-World countries: in California, for example, one of the most profitable cash crops is marijuana, and synthetic or designer drugs can be produced in small suitably equipped laboratories anywhere.

Transporting drugs:

The international drug traffickers would have to cover long distances to sell their drugs on the markets in the USA and Europe, so they have couriers to take them to the different countries. The drugs are transported by ship, plane or lorry/truck to the drug dealers/drug pushers, who sell them to the consumers. The largest profits are made not by the peasants who cultivate and harvest the coca-leaves, but by those who convert the semi-processed leaves into highly-processed cocaine and by those who sell it in the street: the street value of such cocaine is very high.

Drugs are sometimes detected and seized during routine searches of baggage or body searches, although couriers are skilful at finding ways and means of smuggling drugs through customs by hiding them in unlikely places. However, narcotics agents frequently use dogs which have been specially trained to recognize the smell of narcotics in luggage, vehicles etc.

The consumers:

There is an alarming tendency among more and more – mainly young – people to

1. become addicted to drugs (there are tens of thousands of drug addicts in Germany alone);
2. start by using hard drugs (bypassing marijuana and hash);
3. start taking drugs very early (some even at the age of 10 or 12);
4. die of a drug overdose before reaching the age of 30;

coca-leaf	Kokablatt
hemp	Hanf
cannabis [ˈkænəbɪs]	Hanf(pflanze)
poppy seeds	Mohnsamen
'Golden Triangle' [ˈtraɪæŋgl]	das 'Goldene Dreieck'
cultivation	Anbau
cash crop	für den Verkauf bestimmte Anbaufrucht
synthetic [sɪnˈθetɪk]	künstlich, synthetisch
designer drug	synthetische Droge
laboratory [ləˈbɒrətrɪ]	Labor

drug trafficker [ˈtræfɪkə]	Drogenhändler/in
courier [ˈkʊrɪə]	Kurier
drug dealer	Drogenhändler/in
pusher [ˈpʊʃə]	Rauschgifthändler/in, Dealer/in
consumer	Verbraucher/in, Konsument/in
peasant [ˈpeznt]	(Klein-)Bauer/Bäuerin
to harvest	ernten
semi-processed	halbverarbeitet
highly-processed	hochwertig
street value	Marktwert
to seize [siːz]	beschlagnahmen
routine [ruːˈtiːn] **search**	Routineuntersuchung
body search	Leibesvisitation
unlikely	unerwartet, überraschend
narcotics agent [ˈeɪdʒənt]	Rauschgiftfahnder/in

drug addict	Drogenabhängige(r), -süchtige(r)
to bypass	übergehen, umgehen
overdose	Überdosis

5. have easy access to drugs which are supplied in large quantities;
6. take drugs even if they live in small towns or in the country and not in the big cities, where this is more common;
7. mix 'cocktails' to make the intoxicating or narcotic effect (of feeling 'high') stronger and to intensify the euphoric feelings induced by drugs: they take a large dose of a barbiturate and heroin in addition to a number of other pills;
8. switch to cheaper but even more dangerous synthetic drugs, which are also more addictive;
9. commit drug-related crimes to get money to support their habit.

Methods of combating drug abuse:

1. International co-operation: multilateral efforts are essential in the fight against drug abuse.
2. Eradicate local crops of opium poppies, coca and cannabis, confiscate the chemicals used in processing drugs, destroy the laboratories engaged in cocaine processing, locate and destroy the clandestine airstrips in the jungle or in the mountains.
3. Encourage the peasants to find replacement crops such as coffee or cocoa.
4. More determined efforts to get hold of the major drug distributors, the middlemen and the street-level dealers/pushers.
5. More police and customs officers to track down the supplies and to reduce the smuggling of drugs into the consumer countries.
6. More undercover agents who can give the police valuable information about the major drug distributors.
7. Stricter laws against the peddling of drugs and harsher penalties for drug racketeers.
8. Provide more and better information for parents in order to teach them how to keep their children away from drugs (for example the organization of self-help groups).
9. More rehabilitation centres for drug addicts who need to undergo special withdrawal treatment.
10. More research into the psychological and social reasons for drug abuse so that the roots of the problem can be tackled.

to supply	liefern
intoxicating [ɪn'tɒksɪkeɪtɪŋ]	berauschend
euphoric [ju:'fɒrɪk]	euphorisch
to induce	herbeiführen, bewirken
drug-related	mit Drogen in Zusammenhang stehend
to combat ['kɒmbæt]	bekämpfen
multilateral efforts [ˌmʌltɪ'lætərəl]	*hier:* Anstrengungen, die die Zusammenarbeit mehrerer Länder erfordern
to eradicate [ɪ'rædɪkeɪt]	vernichten, ausrotten
to confiscate	beschlagnahmen
to locate	orten
clandestine [klæn'destɪn]	heimlich, geheim
replacement	Ersatz
cocoa ['kəʊkəʊ]	Kakao
distributor [dɪ'strɪbjʊtə(r)]	Verteiler/in
middleman	Zwischenhändler/in
street-level dealer	Straßen-, Kleinhändler/in
to track down	aufspüren
undercover agent ['eɪdʒənt]	(verdeckt ermittelnde[r]) V-Mann/Frau der Polizei
to peddle	handeln mit
racketeer	Gangster, Gauner
self-help group	Selbsthilfegruppe
rehabilitation centre	Rehabilitationszentrum
to undergo s.th.	sich ... unterziehen
withdrawal treatment	Entziehungskur
research	Forschung

Problems:

1. Difficulties in locating and destroying the large cultivation areas in remote regions.
2. The laboratories for processing crude morphine or coca paste are often in the hands of powerful crime syndicates – the 'drug barons' of the international drug cartels are often too powerful to be controlled effectively by the narcotics/drugs squads.
3. Sniffer dogs able to smell drugs, body searches and border checks, although all useful, cannot prevent the trade in drugs entirely.
4. Should 'less dangerous' drugs be legalized and the possession of drugs in small quantities decriminalized?
5. Should doctors be permitted to prescribe special drugs for addicts to prevent them from committing crimes?

remote	abgelegen
crude	Roh-
coca paste [peɪst]	Kokapaste
syndicate ['sɪndɪkət]	Verbrecherring, Syndikat
'drug baron'	'Drogenboss'
cartel [kɑː'tel]	Ring, Kartell
squad [skwɒd]	Dezernat
sniffer dog	Spürhund
to legalize	rechtskräftig machen, legalisieren
to decriminalize	entkriminalisieren
to prescribe	verordnen, verschreiben

The Theatre

Basic information:

The mecca of British theatre-goers is London, which boasts more than 100 professional theatres, many of which are concentrated in the West End and the South Bank. The centre of the theatre scene in the US is Broadway in New York.

New stage productions are presented every year, many of them costing several million pounds or dollars. Production costs, however, are not a guarantee of box-office success. Most large theatres are repertory theatres with a stock company of actors performing a repertoire of plays at these particular theatres only. Provincial theatres are mainly served by touring companies as they usually cannot afford their own repertory companies.

Theatre-goers can look at the bills outside the theatres and decide which play to see. 'Hamlet' may be on at the Old Vic, a serious drama by a contemporary playwright at the Royal Court or an Italian opera at Covent Garden. If the performance or show has not sold out, they can

THE GLOBE THEATRE.

mecca	Zentrum, Anziehungspunkt
theatre-goer	Theaterbesucher/in
to boast something	*hier:* sich rühmen, etwas zu haben
the West End	Theater-, Unterhaltungsviertel von London
stage	Bühne
box-office	Kasse
repertory ['repətərɪ] **theatre**	Theater mit stehender Truppe
stock company	festes Ensemble
actor, actress	Schauspieler/in
to perform	aufführen
repertoire ['repətwɑ:]	Repertoire
play	Theaterstück
touring company	Wanderbühne
repertory company	festes Ensemble
bill	Programm (eines Theaters usw.)
to be on	laufen, gegeben werden
contemporary [kən'tempərərɪ]	zeitgenössisch
playwright	Bühnenschriftsteller/in
opera ['ɒpərə]	Oper
performance	Aufführung
sold out	ausverkauft sein

buy tickets for the stalls, the circle or the gallery at the box-office. Families and tourists often prefer to attend matinée performances in the afternoon.

A career on the stage

People not content with amateur theatricals but interested in becoming professional actors and actresses usually attend a school of acting. An agent may then find them a role/part in a new play, for which they must audition. Actors who have proved suitable at the audition are cast in various roles according to age, sex, ability and experience. The leading man and leading lady have the chief parts, while the juvenile lead is played by a young but gifted actor or actress. There are generally a number of supporting roles. Young, innocent-looking girls are required for ingénue roles, while character actors and actresses specialize in playing eccentric characters.

A small part which requires considerable talent is called a cameo role. Walk-on parts are those of actors who merely appear on stage without speaking. Should a member of the cast fall ill, an understudy who has learned the role takes over.

The players are given their scripts so that they can learn their lines and cues by heart. Rehearsals under the guidance of the director continue until the dress rehearsal just before the play's première/first night. That night everyone suffers from first-night nerves: stage fright, fear of drying up, missing cues etc. Backstage, in the dressing-rooms, actors and actresses put on their costumes and are made up. The director waits in the wings with last-minute stage directions, the stage-manager makes sure that the previously built and painted set/scenery is in place, that the prompter is in position and that the lighting and props are ready. At last the lights dim and the curtain rises; the first scene begins.

stalls [stɔ:lz]	Sperrsitz
circle	Rang
gallery	Galerie
to attend	besuchen
matinée	Nachmittagsvorstellung
on the stage	*hier:* beim Theater
amateur ['æmətə] **theatricals**	Theateraufführungen durch Amateure
school of acting/drama school	Schauspielschule
agent ['eɪdʒənt]	Agent/in
role/part	Rolle
to audition (for a part)	vorsprechen, vorspielen
an audition	Vorsprechen, Vorspielen
to be cast in a role	eine Rolle (zugewiesen) bekommen
leading man/lady	Hauptdarsteller/in
juvenile ['dʒu:vənaɪl] **lead** [li:d]	jugendliche Hauptrolle
gifted	begabt
supporting role	Nebenrolle
ingénue ['æ̃nʒeɪnju:]	die "Naive" (in einem Theaterstück)
character actor/actress	Charakterdarsteller/in
cameo ['kæmɪəʊ]	Miniatur-
walk-on part	Statistenrolle
cast	Besetzung
understudy	Ersatzschauspieler/in
script	Theatermanuskript
lines	Vers, Rolle
cue	Stichwort
rehearsal [rɪ'hɜ:sl]	Probe
director	Regisseur/in, Spielleiter/in
dress rehearsal	Generalprobe
première/first night	Erst-, Uraufführung
stage fright	Lampenfieber
to dry up	steckenbleiben (im Text)
backstage	hinter der Bühne
costumes ['kɒstju:mz]	Kostüme
in the wings	hinter den Kulissen
stage directions	Bühnenanweisungen
stage-manager	Inspizient/in
set/scenery	Bühnenausstattung, Bühnenbild
prompter	Souffleur, Souffleuse
props (pl.)	Requisiten
scene	Auftritt, Szene

When the curtain falls at the end of a successful performance, the performers, who may have to take several curtain calls, are rewarded by the audience with sustained applause, maybe even with a standing ovation. The critics who have attended rush off to write their reviews, in which they praise the actors' interpretation of their parts etc. A play receiving rave reviews invariably becomes a hit/smash.

General problems:

1. Productions are becoming more and more expensive.
2. Theatres both in big cities and in the provinces generally suffer from a chronic shortage of money, partly owing to a lack of public subsidies.
3. Theatre owners and producers are often more interested in profits than in the quality of the plays produced, which leads to a lowering of standards.
4. New talent must be sought and backed.
5. There is a need for more tolerant and open-minded attitudes to experimental techniques like those used in off-Broadway productions and new dramatic modes of presentation e.g. theatre-in-the-round.

curtain call	Hervorruf der Künstler vor den Vorhang als Zeichen des Beifalls
audience	Publikum
sustained	anhaltend
applause [ə'plɔ:z]	Beifall
standing ovation	stürmischer Beifall
critic	Kritiker/in, Rezensent/in
review	Kritik, Rezension
interpretation	Interpretation
rave review	'Bombenkritik'
hit/smash	großer Erfolg

subsidies ['sʌbsɪdɪ:z]	Subventionen
producer	Produzent/in (für die geschäftliche Seite zuständig)
to back	unterstützen
technique [tek'ni:k]	Technik, Methode
off-Broadway	New Yorker Theater, die nicht zu den Broadway-Theatern gehören
theatre-in-the-round	Aufführung, bei der das Publikum rings um die Bühne sitzt

… a marvellous
movie, starring/featuring …
… an outstanding performance,
directed by …, produced by …
… a humorous and touching story,
based on the novel …
… skilfully written,
made with great
professionalism …
… 5 Oscar
nominations …

Films

Basic information:

The film/movie industry has become a multi-billion-dollar business, not only in the USA. Whereas the early films at the beginning of the 20th century were silent movies shot in black and white, films today are mainly with sound and in colour and are presented in 70 mm and Dolby Stereo on the screen. The production of feature films, whether shot in a studio or on location, often costs millions of dollars or pounds.

A film producer and director need a talented cast to make a quality film. Professional actors/actresses are normally preferred to amateurs. Minor parts e.g. in crowd scenes and battle scenes are played by extras hired on a temporary basis. Outstanding films, actresses and actors, cameramen and camerawomen and writers of screenplays/scenarios often receive awards at film festivals (e.g. an 'Oscar'). Such films are usually box-office smashes, while others often turn out to be flops.

There are big-budget films produced by large movie companies (like MGM/United Artists or Columbia Pictures) and low-budget, often independent films. Films are produced, distributed by a distribution company and marketed.

In large countries where English is not spoken a dubbed version or one with subtitles is shown.

movie	Film
starring/featuring ...	mit ... in der Hauptrolle
performance	Darstellung
to direct	Regie führen
novel	Roman
nomination	Nominierung

silent movie	Stummfilm
to shoot	*hier:* drehen
screen	Leinwand
feature(film)	Spielfilm
on location	an Originalschauplätzen
producer	Produzent/in
director	Regisseur/in
cast	Besetzung
actor/actress	Schauspieler/in
amateur ['æmətə]	Amateur
minor part	Nebenrolle
extra	Statist/in
screenplay/scenario	Drehbuch
award [ə'wɔ:d]	Auszeichnung
box-office smash	Kassenschlager
flop	Reinfall
big-budget ['bʌdʒɪt] **film**	ein teurer Film
movie company	Filmgesellschaft
to distribute [dɪ'strɪbju:t]	*hier:* verleihen
to market	vertreiben
to dub	synchronisieren
subtitle	Untertitel

Types of films:

- a silent film/movie
- a (serious) problem film
- a documentary on, for example, wildlife
- a witty comedy
- a film classic or epic, for example a historical film
- a western
- a fantasy or science fiction (sci-fi) film
- an action or adventure film
- a thriller or horror film
- an animated cartoon

Films are generally meant to entertain and, in some cases, enlighten the audiences in the cinemas and the viewers of TV films at home. Some present serious information, others deal with topical and controversial issues and frequently influence public opinion. Provocative films sometimes even cause scandals.

General problems:

1. The film industry is confronted with the task of enticing the public back into the cinemas and of surviving in the face of tough competition from television and the video business, especially as more and more feature films are now being shown on TV.
2. It is often difficult to find producers willing to finance expensive productions.
3. Many producers are interested only in films with great box-office potential rather than ones of artistic value.
4. To guarantee diversity there is a need for financial support for independent film productions.

documentary [ˌdɒkjʊ'mentərɪ]	Dokumentarfilm
epic ['epɪk]	Monumentalfilm
animated cartoon	Zeichentrickfilm
to entertain	unterhalten
to enlighten	aufklären
audience	Zuschauer, Publikum
viewer	Zuschauer/in (am Fernseher)
topical	aktuell
controversial [ˌkɒntrə'vɜːʃəl]	strittig, umstritten, kontrovers
issue ['ɪʃjuː]	Problem, Streitfrage
provocative [prə'vɒkətɪv]	provozierend
scandal	Skandal
to entice	locken
to survive [sə'vaɪv]	überleben
competition	Wettbewerb, Konkurrenz
artistic	künstlerisch
diversity [daɪ'vɜːsətɪ]	Vielfalt

Music

Basic information:

There is a wide range of pop(ular) music (rock, folk, jazz etc.) and classical music (symphonies or chamber music, operas, ballet music etc). As these different categories have various features in common, it is often difficult to draw a clear distinction between them.

The contemporary music scene is very diversified and the audience/following of pop and classical music is enormous. Music has become a multi-billion-dollar business worldwide, so that media and entertainment giants now control the international markets. Often a record company is organized as an entertainment conglomerate with a record music business and interests in TV (e.g. producing and distributing videos). In addition to many smaller labels, there are a few large companies: Bertelsmann Music Group, Warner Communications, CBS, EMI etc.

1. Pop music – the making of a star:

Your musical talent may be discovered early. At six, for example, you may play the recorder, at twelve the piano; you may sing in the school choir and later become the singer or the keyboard player in a band. The other musicians in the band may play the (solo/lead, rhythm or bass) guitar, the saxophone, the drums or other percussion instruments. Your musical style may be influenced by rock'n'roll, hard rock, jazz, disco, country, folk music etc.

Expensive technical equipment (amplifiers, loudspeakers, microphones etc.) is required to produce a good sound. You practise a lot, record your songs and send demo tapes to a record company in the hope of making a contract. If a single, an LP or CD is to be produced in a (24-track) recording studio, you will need a producer, a sound engineer, someone to arrange the songs etc. unless you compose the songs, write the lyrics, arrange the music and produce the record yourself.

If your debut single or album is released and sells well, it may climb the charts (pop singers whose records sell extremely well are rewarded with golden or even platinum records). If you play jazz or pop music, you may have gigs in the concert halls around the country. Once you have made a name for yourself as a musician, you may tour Europe or the

classical	klassisch
symphony ['sɪmfənɪ]	Symphonie
chamber ['tʃeɪmbə] **music**	Kammermusik
opera ['ɒpərə]	Oper
ballet ['bæleɪ]	Ballett
contemporary [kən'tempərərɪ]	gegenwärtig, zeitgenössisch
audience	Hörerschaft
following	Anhängerschaft
giant ['dʒaɪənt]	Riese
to control	beherrschen
record company	Plattenfirma
conglomerate [kən'glɒməreɪt]	Konglomerat, Konzern
to produce	herstellen
to distribute [di'strɪbju:t]	vertreiben
label	Plattenfirma
recorder	Blockflöte
choir ['kwaɪə]	Chor
keyboard	Tasteninstrument, Keyboard
musician [mju:'zɪʃn]	Musiker/in
rhythm ['rɪðəm]	Rhythmus
bass [beɪs]	Baß
drums	Schlagzeug
percussion	Schlaginstrument, Schlagzeug
equipment	Ausrüstung
amplifier	Verstärker
demo tape	Demonstrationsband
contract	Vertrag
CD	Compact Disc
24-track	24-spurig
sound engineer	Tontechniker, -ingenieur
to arrange	arrangieren, bearbeiten
lyrics	Text eines Lieds
debut ['deɪbu:] **single**	erste Single
to release	herausgeben
charts	Hitparade
platinum ['plætɪnəm]	Platin
gig [gɪg]	Auftritt

USA promoting your (latest) LP. Even when you are on tour you will have to rehearse constantly before performing at concerts attended by thousands of fans.

2. Classical music:

Pianists, violinists or cello virtuosos unable to reach the extremely high standards required of soloists may join a symphony orchestra, the most famous of which are the London Symphony Orchestra, the New York Philharmonic Orchestra etc. Performances of works by great composers, e.g. an opus like Beethoven's Seventh Symphony in A major or Brahms' D minor piano concerto are particularly popular.

After attending a concert, a music critic may write about the sensitivity of the conductor's interpretation, about the brilliance of the brass, the precision of the wind, the clarity of the strings, the technique of the soloist, the acoustics of the concert hall and the applause with which the audience expressed its enthusiasm.

General problems:

1. Rock stars often become cult figures or idols, the objects of a personality cult.
2. Synthesizers, rhythm machines etc. are replacing live musicians on stage or in the recording studios.
3. More and more videos are being produced (e.g. for the title-tracks of new LPs) to promote the sales of records.
4. Small independent record labels cannot compete with the media and entertainment giants in the battle for a share in the market.
5. Symphony or chamber orchestras, especially in the provinces, are often lacking in funds, a problem which could be solved by an increase in subsidies.

to promote	werben für
on tour	auf Tournee
to rehearse [rɪ'hɜ:s]	proben
to perform	auftreten
to attend	besuchen
violinist ['vaɪəlɪnɪst]	Geiger/in
virtuoso [ˌvɜ:tjʊ'əʊzəʊ]	Virtuose, Virtuosin
orchestra ['ɔ:kɪstrə]	Orchester
performance	Aufführung
composer	Komponist/in
opus ['əʊpəs]	Werk, Opus
A major	A-Dur
D minor	d-Moll
concerto [kən'tʃeətəʊ]	Konzert
critic	Kritiker/in
sensitivity	Feingefühl, Sensitivität
conductor	Dirigent/in
brass [brɑ:s]	Blechinstrumente, Blechbläser
wind	Blasinstrumente, Bläser
strings	Streichinstrumente, Streicher
technique [tek'ni:k]	Technik, Kunstfertigkeit
acoustics [ə'ku:stɪks]	Akustik
applause [ə'plɔ:z]	Beifall
idol	Idol
synthesizer ['sɪnθɪsaɪzə]	Synthesiser
title-track	Titelsong
to compete with	konkurrieren mit
share	Anteil
funds	Geldmittel
subsidies ['sʌbsɪdi:z]	Subventionen

... Bronze Age artefacts
... Gallo-Roman silver treasures: 250 exhibits from European collections – antique vases and jewellery
... glassware, furniture etc from the Biedermeier period
... woodcut prints by Brueghel the Elder
... the sculptures of the sculptor Henry Moore

Art

Basic information:

Whether they have studied art at an art college or not, artists who have learned certain techniques are then free to develop their own personal styles if they are talented enough to be creative and innovative rather than resort to a derivative style. Various tools and materials are used, e.g. stone, metal or wood by a sculptor, oil-colours, water-colours and brushes by a painter, charcoal for charcoal sketches by a drawer etc. The common aim of all is to produce works of art, preferably masterpieces, many of which are on display in famous galleries like the National Gallery or the Tate Gallery in London and the Guggenheim Museum (the Museum of Modern Art) in New York.

the Bronze [brɒnz] **Age** — Bronzezeitalter
artefact ['ɑ:tɪfækt] — Gebrauchsgegenstand, Gerät, Schmuck
exhibit [ɪg'zɪbɪt] — Ausstellungsstück, Exponat
collection — Sammlung
vase [vɑ:z] — Vase
jewellery ['dʒu:əlrɪ] — Schmuck
woodcut print — Holzschnittdruck
B. the Elder — B. der Ältere
glassware — Glaswaren
sculpture ['skʌlptʃə]/**sculptor** — Plastik, Skulptur/Bildhauer/in

art — Kunst, bes. bildende Kunst
artist — Künstler/in
technique [tek'ni:k] — Technik
creative — schöpferisch, kreativ
innovative ['ɪnəˌveɪtɪv] — bereit, Neuerungen einzuführen; innovativ
derivative [dɪ'rɪvətɪv] — nachahmend, von anderen abgeleitet
oil-colours — Ölfarben
water-colours — Wasserfarben, Aquarell
charcoal — Zeichenkohle, Kohlestift
sketch — Skizze
drawer ['drɔ:ə] — Zeichner/in
work of art — Kunstwerk
masterpiece — Meisterwerk
to be on display/to display — ausgestellt sein/ausstellen
gallery — Galerie

Exhibitions at art galleries include works displayed in permanent collections: oil paintings, water-colours, landscapes, seascapes, (self-)portraits, still lifes, drawings, collages, and graphics by graphic artists. In addition to permanent collections there are also loan-collections of objects of art on loan to museums and galleries.

Art lovers with good taste and an aesthetic sense can become connoisseurs of such artistic achievements as Norman arches, Gothic cathedrals, Baroque architecture, the landscape paintings of the Impressionists, the rich colours of the Expressionists, the geometric designs of the Cubists, decorative Art Deco, the flowing lines and bright colours of Art Nouveau, the surrealist paintings of Dali, the pop art of the 1960s, Post-Modernism, and abstract art in its many forms.

Fostering art today

Young aspiring artists who have not yet won recognition have difficulty in finding a 'market-place', for example in commercial galleries. Patronage of the arts by private patrons or sponsorship by firms as well as an increase in public subsidies could help artists financially and thus foster art in general. Furthermore, interest in and appreciation of the fine arts can only really grow if works are made accessible to the general public and not just to a cultured minority.

exhibition	Ausstellung
portrait ['pɔ:trɪt]	Bildnis, Porträt
still life	Stilleben
drawing ['drɔ:ɪŋ]	Zeichnung
collage [kɒ'lɑ:ʒ]	Collage
graphics *pl*	Graphik, graphische Kunst
loan-collection	Wanderausstellung
aesthetic [i:s'θetɪk] **sense**	Sinn für das Schöne
connoisseur [ˌkɒnə'sɜ:]	(Kunst-)Kenner
artistic	künstlerisch, Kunst-
Norman arch [ɑ:tʃ]	normannischer Bogen
Gothic ['gɒθɪk]	gotisch, die Gotik
Baroque [bə'rɒk]	barock, das Barock
architecture ['ɑ:kɪtektʃə]	Baukunst, Architektur
Art Nouveau [ˌɑ:rnu:'vəʊ]	Jugendstil

to foster	fördern
aspiring	hochstrebend, ehrgeizig
recognition	Anerkennung
patronage ['pætrənɪdʒ]	Mäzenatentum, Förderung
patron ['peɪtrən]	Gönner, Förderer, Mäzen
sponsorship	finanzielle Förderung (meist) durch Privatfirmen
subsidies ['sʌbsɪdɪ:z]	Subventionen
the (fine) arts	die bildenden/schönen Künste
cultured	kultiviert, gebildet

Literature

Drama – Poetry – Narrative prose

Literature can be divided into three main categories, i.e. drama, poetry and narrative prose, all of which can, in turn, be subdivided into various genres like the tragedy, the sonnet, the novel, the short story etc. Literary criticism is concerned with analysing, interpreting and judging works of literature. However, it does not take a critic to distinguish between good poetry and doggerel, a major novel (especially a classic) and a pot-boiler.

I. Drama

British drama can be traced back to the medieval mystery plays, which were concerned with biblical themes, and the morality plays of the fifteenth and sixteenth centuries, which showed man torn between the forces of good and evil. The heyday of British drama was the Elizabethan age, which brought forth such great dramatists as Shakespeare, Marlowe and Jonson. A serious setback was suffered under the Puritans, who were opposed to the theatre. Since the Restoration, however, the creativity of playwrights has produced a wide variety of dramatic works, some of them masterpieces. American contributions, especially in this century, have provided the theatre with a wealth of new ideas, techniques etc.

Tragedy – serious plays with sad endings and complex plots, often including sub-plots – is the most noble branch of drama. Tragic dramatists/tragedians like Shakespeare deal with the inexorable fall of the great and mighty, of kings, generals etc. Their hubris and tragic flaws, which are usually also the theme of the plays, e.g. Othello's jealousy and Macbeth's ambition, cause tragic heroes and heroines to disturb the natural order of things, which only their downfall and destruction can restore. The fate of the protagonists arouses pity and fear in the audience, thus bringing about a catharsis of these emotions.

Tragedies normally consist of five acts, each made up of several scenes.

category	Gruppe, Kategorie
narrative ['nærətɪv] **prose**	Erzählprosa
genre ['ʒɑ:nrə]	Gattung, Genre
tragedy ['trædʒɪdɪ]	Trauerspiel, Tragödie
sonnet	Sonett
novel	Roman
literary criticism	Literaturwissenschaft, -kritik
to interpret [ɪn'tɜ:prɪt]	deuten, interpretieren
critic	Kritiker/in
doggerel	minderwertiges Gedicht
classic	Meisterwerk, Klassiker
pot-boiler	schnell u. schlecht geschriebenes Buch

medieval [ˌmedɪ'i:vl]	mittelalterlich
mystery play	Mysterienspiel
morality play	Moralität
heyday	Höhepunkt, Blütezeit
dramatist	Bühnendichter, Dramatiker
the Restoration	Zeit der Restauration in GB (nach 1660)
playwright	Bühnendichter, Dramatiker
variety [və'raɪətɪ]	Vielfalt
masterpiece	Meisterwerk
technique [tek'ni:k]	Technik
plot	Handlung
sub-plot	Nebenhandlung
tragic dramatist	Tragiker
tragedian [trə'dʒi:djən]	Tragiker
hubris ['hju:bris]	freche Selbstüberhebung, Hybris
flaw	Fehler, Makel
tragic hero	tragischer Held
heroine ['herəʊɪn]	Heldin
protagonist [prəu'tægənɪst]	Hauptfigur, Held/in
audience	Publikum
catharsis [kə'θɑ:sɪs]	innere Reinigung, Katharsis
act	Aufzug, Akt
scene	Szene, Auftritt

The dramatic conflict is developed in five steps:

- exposition
- complication
- climax
- falling action
- resolution

These five steps correspond with the five acts.

Soliloquies (monologues) reveal the feelings and plans of the main characters and release from tension is provided by the comic relief typical of Shakespeare's tragic works. Dramatic (tragic) irony is a device frequently used: the audience understands the implication and meaning of a situation or of the words uttered, while the characters themselves are still in ignorance.

English dramatists seldom heed the unities of time and place, but normally aim at unity of action, which means that everything said and done in the play must be directed towards the one main action.

The chasm between tragedy and comedy is bridged by problem plays by playwrights like Ibsen, which have tragic features but, unlike tragedy, are about ordinary people. History plays deal with historical persons, usually kings, but are not tragic, while the tragicomedy combines tragic and comic elements.

The aim of comedies, with their happy conclusions, is to amuse the audience, often by presenting ridiculous characters and incidents. Traditionally, comedies are about humble and private people, frequently with laughable and exaggerated vices, as in Molière's satirical comedies or comedies of morals. Comedies are sometimes bawdy, make use of such rhetorical figures as hyperbole and often provoke laughter with their play on words e.g. puns.

The large variety of comedies includes the comedy of manners, which satirizes social life, black comedy, which shows tragic aspects of life in a comic way, drawing-room comedy, sentimental comedy, romantic comedy and domestic comedy. The most frivolous kinds are burlesque and farce.

One of the more recent vogues in drama is the Theatre of the Absurd, which includes works by Beckett, Pinter and others.

exposition	Exposition
complication	steigende Handlung
climax ['klaımæks]	Höhepunkt, Umschwung
falling action	fallende Handlung
resolution	Lösung
soliloquy [sə'lıləkwı]	Selbstgespräch
character	Figur (i. einem Drama, Roman etc.)
comic relief	Erholung/Entspannung durch eine komische Szene
dramatic irony	dramatische Ironie
device [dı'vaıs]	(Stil)Mittel
unity of time and place	Einheit von Zeit und Ort
chasm ['kæzəm]	Kluft
history play	histor. Drama, Historienspiel
tragicomedy	Tragikomödie
exaggerated [ıg'zædʒəreıtəd]	übertrieben
bawdy	unzüchtig, obszön
rhetorical figure	rhetorische Sprachfigur
hyperbole [haı'pɜ:bəlı]	Übertreibung, Hyperbel
play on words	Wortspielerei
pun	Wortspiel
comedy of manners	Sittenkomödie
to satirize	satirisch behandeln
drawing-room comedy	Gesellschafts-, Konversationsstück
domestic comedy	bürgerliches Lustspiel
burlesque [bɜ:'lesk]	Posse, Burleske
farce	Posse, Schwank
vogue [vəʊg]	Entwicklung, Trend
Theatre of the Absurd [əb'sɜ:d]	Absurdes Theater

II. Poetry

Major and minor poets and poetesses use poems as a medium for communicating their thoughts, feelings and personal experiences to the reader or to the audience at a poetry reading. The British Poet Laureate has the additional task of composing poems for state occasions. Poetry may be written in free verse (without regular rhythm or rhyme), in blank verse (lines of usually ten syllables without rhyme) or in rhyme. Poems are often divided up into stanzas consisting of a variable number of lines, which may or may not rhyme.

Figurative language, i.e. such imagery as metaphors, similes, symbols and personification, enhances a poem's beauty. Personification is particularly important in allegories, in which, for example, virtues and vices are personified. Other common devices are alliteration and assonance. Poetic licence gives a poet great freedom: he can exploit all the connotations of words and also ignore collocations by replacing these combinations of words commonly used together with startling and unconventional combinations.

With some exceptions, e.g. the sonnet, which consists of fourteen lines with rhymes arranged according to a limited number of fixed schemes, the poet himself can determine the length of his poem. Milton's 'Paradise Lost', which has over ten thousand lines, is an extreme case. Poets enjoy similar freedom in their choice of the type of poem best suited to their theme and intention: lyrics (lyric poetry), narrative poems, ballads, dramatic poetry, pastoral poetry, symbolist poetry, odes, elegies, eulogies and epic poetry.

III. Narrative prose: the novel

Although most prose written today is non-fiction, there is also considerable demand for works of fiction in prose. Two genres that are great favourites with the reading public are the short story and the novel. Novels are book-length stories.

poet	Dichter, Lyriker
poetess	Dichterin, Lyrikerin
poem	Gedicht
poetry reading	Dichterlesung
Poet Laureate ['lɔːrɪət] *(GB)*	Hofdichter
to compose	verfassen, dichten
rhythm ['rɪðəm]	Rhythmus
rhyme	Reim
blank verse	Blankvers
syllable ['sɪləbl]	Silbe
stanza ['stænzə]	Strophe
line	Vers(zeile)
to rhyme	sich reimen
figurative ['fɪgjʊrətɪv] **language**	bildhafte Sprache
imagery ['ɪmɪdʒərɪ]	Bilder, Bildersprache
metaphor ['metəfə]	bildhafter Ausdruck, Metapher
simile ['sɪmɪlɪ]	Vergleich (mit "like" oder "as")
personification	Verkörperung, Personifizierung
to enhance [ɪn'hɑːns]	vergrößern, steigern
allegory	Sinnbild, Allegorie
alliteration	Stabreim, Alliteration
assonance	vokal. Gleichklang, Assonanz
poetic licence	dichterische Freiheit
to exploit	*hier:* ausnutzen
connotation	Nebenbedeutung
collocation	Zusammenstellung, Kollokation
scheme [skiːm]	Schema, System
theme	Stoff, Thema, Gegenstand
lyric	lyrisches Gedicht
narrative poem	Erzählgedicht
pastoral poetry	Schäferlyrik, -dichtung
ode	Ode
elegy ['elɪdʒɪ]	Klagelied
eulogy ['juləd͡ʒɪ]	Lobpreisung
epic poetry	epische Dichtung

non-fiction	Sachliteratur, -texte
fiction	Dichtung/Erzählungs-, Prosa-, Romanliteratur
reading public	Lesepublikum, Leserschaft

The main ingredients of a novel are plot, characters, action and incident. A good novelist must fulfil certain conditions: the development of his characters must be convincing, these characters must be round and not flat, the plot must arouse curiosity and suspense, the action must be set in a place and time of interest to the reader and the style should be vivid, not insipid.

Apart from that, an author has almost unlimited freedom: he can decide whether to use a first-person narrator or a third-person narrator such as an omniscient narrator or an observer-narrator. He can choose the point(s) of view he prefers, e.g. a limited point of view or a shifting point of view.

All kinds of stylistic devices are at his disposal: satire, irony, understatement, imagery etc. He need not develop the plot chronologically but can, instead, use flashbacks and anticipation, especially in a novel with time as its theme (the time novel). A novel's setting can be exotic or familiar, the past (historical novels) or the future (science fiction novels). In the portrayal of the heroes and heroines (or anti-heroes and anti-heroines), the novelist can give insight into their characters by means of their actions, the ideas, feelings and opinions expressed in dialogues and the depiction of the social and cultural backgrounds that have moulded them. This makes it easier for the reader to identify with them. One method for revealing the characters' innermost feelings, psychological make-up and emotional life is the 'stream of consciousness' technique or interior monologue, which was perfected by James Joyce in his novel 'Ulysses'.

Some examples of the many types of novel are: the epistolary novel, the sentimental novel, the Gothic novel, the saga (or chronicle novel), the picaresque novel, the key novel, the comic novel, the detective novel ('whodunit'), the spy novel, the thriller, the novel of adventure and, last but not least, the anti-novel.

IV. Narrative prose: the short story

Like the novel, the short story is an example of prose fiction, though it is, as the name implies, shorter. Unlike the novel, it normally restricts itself to one event or theme only. Other examples of short works of prose fiction, precursors of the short story, are myths, legends, parables from the

ingredient [ɪn'gri:djənt]	Bestandteil, Merkmal
novelist	Romanschriftsteller(in)
round	lebendig, komplex, lebensecht
flat	stereotyp (Gegent.v. "round")
suspense	Spannung
to be set in	als Schauplatz haben
vivid	lebendig, bunt
insipid	fad, schal, farblos
first-person narrator	Ich-Erzähler
omniscient [ɒm'nɪsɪənt] **narrator**	allwissender Erzähler
observer-narrator	Erzähler als berichtender Augenzeuge, Protokollant
point of view	Standpunkt
shifting	wechselnd
stylistic device	Stilmittel
understatement	Untertreibung
flashback	Rückblende
anticipation	Vorgriff, Vorwegnahme
setting	Schauplatz, Handlungsraum
science fiction novel	Zukunftsroman
portrayal	Schilderung
dialogue ['daɪəlɒg]	Dialog
depiction	Beschreibung, Schilderung
to mould	formen
to identify with s.o.	sich mit jmd. identifizieren
make-up	*hier:* Veranlagung, Natur
stream of consciousness/interior monologue ['mɒnəlɒg]	Bewußtseinsstrom, innerer Monolog
epistolary novel	Briefroman
saga ['sɑ:gə]	Familienroman
picaresque [ˌpɪkə'resk] **novel**	Schelmenroman, pikaresker R.
key novel	Schlüsselroman
detective novel, crime novel	Detektiv-, Kriminalroman
whodunit [ˌhu:'dʌnɪt]	"Krimi"
spy novel	Spionageroman
precursor	Vorläufer
parable ['pærəbl]	Gleichnis, Parabel

Bible, fairy stories, fables, anecdotes etc. Although the term 'short story' became common only towards the end of the nineteenth century, the actual genre was originated by E. A. Poe in America before the middle of the nineteenth century. Thanks to its readability and flexibility, it has since flourished, particularly in North America, which has brought forth many great story-tellers.

The brevity of the short story naturally determines its characteristics. There is not enough room either for a complicated plot or for an in-depth portrayal of characters and their development. In the 'plot story' typical of the 19th century a simple plot leads straight to the crisis, climax and denouement (resolution), while the 'plotless story' typical of the 20th century even dispenses with a plot and a long exposition entirely and has an open ending. The writer of a plotless story concentrates on a 'slice of life' in order to demonstrate how the protagonist reacts to a certain important event or situation, usually at a critical time in his or her life. The writer's main concern is to throw light on the situation and show the change(s) the character undergoes as a result of what he has learnt, felt, gone through etc. This is especially true of the stories of initiation, which deal with 'revelation and evolution' as experienced by, in most cases, young people.

The author has a wide choice of narrative techniques, e.g. observer-narrators, first-person narrators and omniscient narrators. Although the lack of strict rules partly explains the popularity of this genre, a good short-story writer should, according to literary scholars, fulfil certain conditions, e.g. a dense atmosphere, 'unity of effect' where structure is concerned and, above all, the ability to express himself clearly in a condensed and plain style. To avoid superfluous words, the writer must resort to 'allusion' and 'omission', simply hinting at things and leaving out anything unnecessary. The typical protagonists are not outstanding in any way: they are either ordinary citizens leading everyday lives in the real world or people living on the fringes of society, e.g. loners, outsiders, eccentrics or social misfits.

fairy story (fairy tale)	Märchen
term	Begriff
readability	Lesbarkeit
to flourish ['flʌrɪʃ]	blühen, gedeihen
brevity	Kürze
in-depth	gründlich, in die Tiefe gehend
crisis	Krise
climax	Höhepunkt
dénouement [deɪ'nu:mɒŋ]	Ausgang, Entscheidung, Lösung
resolution	Lösung des Knotens
to dispense with	verzichten auf
exposition	Exposition
open ending	offener Schluß
'slice of life'	repräsentativer Lebensausschnitt
initiation	Einführung, Aufnahme
revelation	Enthüllung, Offenbarung
evolution	Entwicklung
literary scholar ['skɒlə]	Literaturwissenschaftler
dense	verdichtet, dicht
condensed	komprimiert, verdichtet
plain	schlicht, einfach
superfluous [su:'pɜ:flʊəs]	überflüssig
allusion	Andeutung, Anspielung
omission	Auslassung, Weglassung
to hint at	anspielen auf
on the fringes [frɪndʒ]	am Rande
loner	Einzelgänger
misfit	schlecht angepaßter Mensch

Index